Being Together
Unitarians Cele
Congregational Life

Edited by Matthew F. Smith

The Lindsey Press
London

Published by The Lindsey Press
on behalf of the General Assembly of Unitarian and Free
Christian Churches,
Essex Hall, 1–6 Essex Street, London WC2R 3HY, UK

ISBN 0 85319 073 9

Typeset by Garth Stewart, Oxford

Printed and bound in the United Kingdom by Lightning
Source, Milton Keynes

Contents

Part Two: Being together in the wider community

Part Three: New ways of being together

Part Four: Growing congregations

Appendix

Introduction

Matthew F. Smith

This new collection of essays is, in some senses, a successor to *Prospects for the Unitarian Movement*, published in 2002. Once again, Unitarian contributors, both ministers and laypeople, have taken up the challenge to tackle a topic suggested to them by the editor – each chapter addressing a theme that readers will, it is hoped, recognise as highly relevant to the present circumstances of Unitarianism in the United Kingdom. As in the earlier book, each chapter ends with a short set of questions that are intended to stimulate group discussion, thus providing a second, and perhaps equally rewarding, use for the book.

While *Prospects* was wide ranging in its scope, this new production is somewhat more narrowly focused – concentrating on congregations as the most visible and concrete manifestation of what it is to belong to the Unitarian community. Congregational life is undoubtedly a many-faceted phenomenon. To do the subject justice, being together in religious fellowship needs to be explored through many dimensions and to be viewed from a range of magnifications.

Our investigation requires more than merely recounting the activities of congregations – such as worship and small-group work – and attempting to assess the value or success of these elements. We need to be prepared to zoom close up and think about the life of a congregation in terms of the interaction between individuals: their personal motivations and their ability to listen to one another. Furthermore, we need the panoramic view that comprehends the congregation as a feature within the local landscape, existing in a dynamic relationship with its

Assembly (presented in the Appendix to this book) is, in some senses, an attempt to articulate shared values for the movement without hobbling the individual conscience. Only time will tell how valuable or significant this document will prove to be.

Chapters in this book touch upon the Christian foundations of our ideas about being a liberal religious congregation, but they also highlight the increasing diversity of British society, in terms of both cultural backgrounds and personal interests, which challenge congregations to consider the changes they may need to make in order to be recognised as places of welcome for 21st-century people.

For me as editor, the *leitmotif* that runs through the essays is the idea that the exploration and experience of being in compassionate relationship with other human beings constitutes a huge part of what it means to be religious. Maybe this is especially so in a non-credal faith community, where assent to the worship of a transcendent Deity is not required as a condition of membership. For Unitarians, dogmatic theism does not equate to the true religious spirit. Rather, to be a Unitarian entails constant questioning. There is a sense that neither the solitary spiritual quest nor the fellowship of family life can encompass all that the religious life is meant to involve. There must be a communal dimension to faith, and an engagement with society based on concern for the other. Unitarians point out that service to others is a duty prescribed in all of the major faith traditions, while religious fellowship at its best strengthens the individual for life's journey – at the same time weaving the fabric of community.

I should like to put on record my enormous gratitude to Catherine Robinson for painstakingly copy-editing this book and for working so tirelessly with all the authors, and my thanks also to the members of the General Assembly's Publications Panel, to our indefatigable band of writers, and to all those who helped them in any way in turning sometimes elusive ideas into such substantive, challenging, and thought-provoking material. I hope that at least some elements in this book will resonate with you, and inspire you to find paths of service and spiritual enrichment based on religious fellowship that is tolerant, accepting, and welcoming of diversity.

Part One
Enriching the life of our congregations

1 A Unitarian church: its nature and purpose

Clifford M. Reed

What is distinctive about a church – a meeting, fellowship, or congregation – that is a member of the General Assembly of Unitarian and Free Christian Churches? This is a necessary question, for while we have our own unique history and cherished heritage, what matters is the role that we play within the contemporary religious spectrum. A congregation may extend friendship, co-operation, and goodwill to other communities of faith, but what content does it bring to the relationship? What is unique about the spiritual ground on which it stands? What is the basis for its participation in the dialogue and interchange of a multi-faith society? What does it have to offer to the spiritual hunger of a shallow and secularised culture? We cannot leave our role unexamined. So, what is a Unitarian congregation, or what should it be? What follows, although based on my experience, is necessarily tinged with the ideal!

The church as community

A Unitarian congregation is a community. It is a coming together of individuals and families in something that enfolds and transcends – but does not deny – their individuality and distinctiveness. It is where they gather to be one, celebrating that oneness while respecting and celebrating their inevitable diversity. What it is not, and cannot healthily be, is a uniform collective, subject to the will of one individual or ruling clique. And neither is it a random assemblage of individuals who feel no connectedness among themselves, no sense of belonging or obligation to each other. While a congregation will inevitably have associated with it some who have not made the transition to full participation (or have not yet made it), it will have at its core a group who constitute the true community, for whom the congregation is 'us', rather than 'you' or 'them'.

But Unitarians have no monopoly on community. That is not enough in itself to distinguish our congregations. Indeed, we share with other religious bodies the important task of providing community in an increasingly atomised society where most traditional ties are breaking down. Offering a sense of community is one of the most valuable things that all churches can do; but what is different about the kind of community that we offer?

A distinctive ethos

Jonalu Johnstone, a minister in our American sister denomination, wrote this:

> In Unitarian Universalist congregations we gather in community to support our individual spiritual journeys. We trust that openness to one another's experiences will enhance our understanding of our own links with the divine, with our history, and with one another.

These words are an excellent introduction to the ethos that we, as Unitarians and Free Christians, hold dear, if not sacred. It is an ethos that offers an unconditional welcome to all people of goodwill. It says 'welcome', regardless of a person's national, ethnic, religious, or cultural background, or their social class or sexual orientation. It is grounded in respect for the divine / human essence in all people. It is willing to see beyond the accidental and the incidental to the essential. It is open to all who come in search of fellowship, solace, or simply infor-mation. And crucially, it is an ethos that says 'welcome' to the distinctive personal faith and belief systems that people bring with them. Recognising that in each case this is the result of their unique life's journey so far, we neither judge their deepest and most positive experiences nor condemn or belittle their doubts and questionings. Ours is an ethos that lays down no conditions for fellowship, save that of extending to others the same respect and reverence that one seeks and asks for oneself.

A faith community

A Unitarian congregation is a faith community with a distinctive faith. Many people interpret 'faith' as the holding of particular beliefs and adhering to specific creeds, doctrines, confessions, dogmas, or theological propositions; but this is a misapprehension. When it comes to the grand propositions of theology and metaphysics, it is our Unitarian tradition to stand in awe and wonder before the Great Mystery, rather than say too much about it. The members of a Unitarian church will not claim to have full knowledge or a monopoly on truth. Nor will they accept anyone else's claim to do so! Our limited words and concepts cannot capture the infinities or intricacies of the cosmic Process, of which we ourselves are but momentary incarnations. Our faith lies rather in the humble assurance that we belong in this universe – that life's meaning and purpose are forged in the outworking of our unique potential as creative, spiritual beings. Our faith affirms that there is a uniting bond between all people, all creation, if only we can feel it and manifest it in our life together. It is a faith experienced in loving community, but not readily pinned down or defined.

A questing community

A Unitarian community may share in such faith as this, and hold to it despite differences of belief or of language about belief, but this does not mean that it has no interest in searching further. Seeking knowledge, asking (and answering) questions, exploring the as yet unknown – all these are part of its life. It remains a distinctive and inviolate part of the Unitarian tradition to afford a crucial place to reason, the intellect, and the scientific method. A Unitarian congregation may not be a place for cold, impersonal, academic debate, but neither is it a place where the mind is despised or abandoned. Reason's critical role in 'testing the spirits' (I John 4:1) and guiding emotions, in checking the impulse to unreason, is recognised and valued. Although a Unitarian congregation welcomes new promptings of intuition and spirit, it also maintains its traditional respect for the role of reason within faith. As we are fond of saying: you don't have to leave your mind at the door when you come in!

A liberal religious community

A religion – any religion – might be defined as an apparently comprehensive, holistic, and coherent system of belief, values, and practice that binds people together in community. The Unitarian and Free Christian movement, in its constituent congregations, accords with this definition. But we who are part of it define ourselves more specifically as 'liberal religious'. Liberal religion might be called a 'porous' system, meaning that it is open to change and to new insight, both spiritual and intellectual, as opposed to the 'sealed' system of illiberal religion. The liberal church is willing to accept the challenge and stimulation of innovation and criticism. It accepts the possibility of error in long-hallowed 'truths'. For all the discomfort of uncertainty, we think it healthier to be open to the impulses and promptings of the Spirit that 'blows where it wills' (John 3: 8) than to shut out all contrary winds. In the words of the seventeenth-century divine, John Fairfax:

> Thus should we open the door; but if we stop our ear, harden our heart, quench the Spirit, stifle its motions; what is this but to turn the Holy Ghost out of doors?

The liberal Christian tradition

The democratically agreed Object of the Unitarian denomination includes the statement that we 'uphold the liberal *Christian* tradition' [my italics]. However much a congregation may value theological diversity, spiritual pluralism, and openness to the insights of other religious and ethical traditions, liberal Christianity is likely to be where it is rooted, both spiritually and historically. To borrow a metaphor from Isaiah (51:1), that is the rock from which we were hewn, the quarry from which we were cut. There is a clear continuity between the liberal Christian tradition and the other principal positions likely to be held by the members of a Unitarian congregation, such as universalism, religious humanism, and an earth-centred spirituality. In particular, the model of human relationships, the example of personal living, and the vision of a global commonwealth that we owe to Jesus and the Christian tradition at its best remain central to our ideals and witness. And this remains the case even when we are scarcely aware of the debt ourselves!

Liberal Christianity is focused primarily on meeting human need, believing that 'the sabbath was made for man, not man for the sabbath' (Mark 2: 27). It is more concerned with the natural than the supernatural, affirming love's power to transform, renew, and redeem human lives in this world, as Jesus did. He is our brother. We can share his spirit and strive to follow his example. Lester Mondale, Unitarian Universalist minister and signatory of both the 'Humanist Manifesto' (1933) and 'Humanism and its Aspirations' (2003), put it this way:

> We discovered...the truth...that underlies the emphasis of Jesus upon first getting into right relationship with one's fellow men – forgiving them, loving them, helping them – before one can feel right with the world or with what he called the Father in Heaven.

In a Unitarian church, then, this profound emphasis on human need is likely to be seen as the essential spirit of Christianity, and it remains a source of strength and guidance. The liberal church is a setting where the stories and teachings of the Judaeo-Christian heritage can be rediscovered and explored anew. It is a community in dynamic relationship with its liberal Christian roots, yet open also to all that human beings have learned on the universal spiritual journey. With respect for what others hold sacred, and not treating their spiritual treasures as a convenient source of plunder, a Unitarian and Free Christian congregation recognises that the paths of faith and wisdom run through many lands and cultures.

A worshipping community

Whatever else it may be, a Unitarian church is a worshipping community. In worship, its members find self-transcendence in praise and thanksgiving. They may be lifted, without undue drama, into a state of being and of consciousness that sees reality from a new perspective and in which the soul is refreshed. Worship is also a setting where the inner life is quickened in prayer and meditation, where insight and solace are found in words of wisdom and beauty. In worship, life is celebrated and considered, shared hopes and ideals are affirmed, and both comfort and challenge are to be found, according to need. And we do need to worship! Without it, human life loses a crucial dimension. At its best, the worship of a Unitarian and Free Christian congregation is welcoming, accessible, intelligent, inclusive, and spiritual. It respects the individual conscience. It connects us with each other, with the wider world, and with God – the Divine Unity and ground of our being.

Of course, other concerns and activities may characterise the life of a Unitarian and Free Christian congregation, such as social witness and distinctive programmes of religious education for both children and adults, but these are dependent on the core of liberal and committed worship.

A loving community

Every Unitarian and Free Christian congregation is called to be a loving community. This is the vocation of any religious grouping with its roots in the Christian tradition. As Paul wrote, 'If I had all faith...and yet no love, I were nothing' (I Corinthians 13: 2). And this remains the case regardless of how, theologically or intellectually, its members may define or identify the Source of Love. To be a loving community is to foster relationships of kindness, courtesy, respect, and mutual concern within the congregation, so that love pervades its life at every level. And it must reach out further. The loving community looks beyond its own narrow bounds and extends its concern for human welfare into the wider society of which it is part. With people of all faiths, with all people of goodwill, the Unitarian and Free Christian congregation witnesses to the world's need for justice, peace, and compassion.

Acknowledgements

I thank Revd Jonalu Johnstone of First Unitarian Church, Oklahoma City, for giving permission to use her words; Jane Greer, Managing Editor, *UU World*, for her help and advice; Beacon Press for permission to use the quotation by Lester Mondale, and Michelle Corcoran, their Rights and Marketing Associate, for her assistance.

Sources and references

Fairfax, J. (1700) *Primitiae Synagogae: A Sermon Preached at Ipswich, April 26 1700. At the Opening of a New Erected Meeting-House,* London: Tho. Parkhurst

Johnstone, J. (2003) 'Reflections', *UU World: Magazine of the Unitarian Universalist Association,* vol. XVII, no. 6, November/December 2003

Mondale, R. L. (1946) *Three Unitarian Philosophies of Religion,* Boston: Beacon Press

The author

Revd Clifford Reed has been an active Unitarian since his youth. He entered the ministry after working as a librarian in Bolton, in Guyana (with Voluntary Service Overseas), and at Dr Williams's Library in London. Cliff has served the congregations in Ipswich, Framlingham, and Bedfield in Suffolk since 1976. He served the International Council of Unitarians and Universalists as Secretary (1995–97) and Executive Committee member (until 2003). He was the 1997/98 President of the General Assembly of Unitarian and Free Christian Churches. Cliff has contributed hymns and prayers to several collections and written his own books of devotional and worship material: *We Are Here; The Way of the Pilgrim; Celebrating the Flame;* and *Spirit of Time and Place.* His other publications include *Unitarian? What's That? Questions and Answers About a Liberal Religious Alternative,* and, as editor, *A Martyr Soul Remembered: Commemorating the 450th Anniversary of the Death of Michael Servetus.*

Questions for reflection and discussion

1. What is your response to the statement that '*a Unitarian church affirms the value of the distinctive personal faith and belief system of each person*'? How would you respond to a militant atheist, a Creationist fundamentalist, or a Satanist who wanted to become a member?

2. How do you respond to the author's description of the liberal church as 'a community in dynamic relationship with its liberal Christian roots, yet also open to all that human beings have learned on the universal spiritual journey'?

3. Do you distinguish between your beliefs and your faith? Do you have a faith that has survived changing beliefs? Is there a faith that you can share with others when your specific beliefs differ?

2 Worshipping together

Peter Hewis

What makes worshipping together meaningful? Only individuals can answer this question for themselves, but personally I would include the following elements: a sense of the eternal; content that appeals to both the heart and the mind; and a sense of belonging to a caring, sharing community.

Before trying to define worship, let us look at what some individuals have to say about worshipping together: a Cockney woman in east London who had lived through the blitz of World War II, a prosperous manufacturer in the Midlands, and a university vice-chancellor. Each of them has experienced something of great value in a Unitarian community at worship.

The Cockney woman often used to say, 'This hour together on Sundays keeps me going for the rest of the week'. The manufacturer often says, 'Coming here makes such a difference to my daily work and life. My chapel keeps me going.' As for the university vice-chancellor, he regularly said, 'I don't come here for a university lecture. I come for beauty, peace, and worship; for some inspiration to take me forward into the week ahead.'

A Jewish story is relevant here. Mr Adler and Mr Finkel went to their synagogue one day, and the Rabbi asked them, 'Why do you come to synagogue?' Mr Adler replied: 'I come to talk and listen to God'. Mr Finkel replied: 'I come to talk and listen to Mr Finkel!' In their own way, each of those men gave something and received something from attending their synagogue – and maybe that is enough for many people.

In every Unitarian congregation that I have ever known, I have experienced those qualities and attributes that for me typify congregational worship at its best: thinking, feeling, sharing, and a sense of the eternal. I will give three examples that in my view constituted acts of worship.

First I think of a railway worker in a Lancashire town, who often conducted the service in his local chapel when no one else was available to lead it. One Sunday evening, his address was based on three items that he had read in the Sunday paper that morning: the birth of triplets, a suicide, and the sixtieth wedding anniversary of two celebrities. In turn, he looked at each situation and offered his own thoughts about the joys and sorrows involved. He was an ordinary working person, struggling to make sense of life and of God, and for me the service was congregational worship at its best. *It appealed to the intellect and made us all think about our own lives.*

Secondly I remember leading worship in an old Meeting House in Sussex, when I was asked to announce that a distant member of the congregation had died. People remained seated at the end of the service while the elderly pianist played 'Nimrod' in memory of the deceased member, who had been greatly loved. As she played, the old pianist had tears streaming down her cheeks and hit a few wrong notes, but everyone in that congregation was moved by the music, offered as a tribute to the memory of a friend. *That worship appealed to the emotions, and evoked the sense of belonging to a sharing community.*

Thirdly I recall sitting in a chapel surrounded by industrial buildings and looking at the quality of the artefacts in the chapel: wonderful warm-coloured oak panelling and embroideries of apple trees, lovingly crafted by a previous generation of women in memory of a mother and grand-mother, creating in the process a remarkable symbol of life and faith. On that day, it seemed to me that the whole world was a unity, one that included the world of nature, the world of humankind, and the world of the spirit. *That personal worship appealed to my sense of the eternal.* I have had similar experiences in a Liberal Jewish synagogue in Tennessee, in a mosque in Cyprus, in a Catholic church on the edge of the North African desert, and in a Quaker Meeting House in Warwickshire. In each case, although the experience was very personal, it took place in the context of a worshipping community.

Can worship be defined?

Many attempts have been made over the years: here are some definitions taken from dictionaries, from three Unitarian ministers, and from the Society of Friends.

- The *Oxford Concise Dictionary*:
  (Worth ship): Respect or honour shown to a person or thing (circa 1610).
  Reverence or veneration paid to a being or power regarded as supernatural or divine; the action or practice of displaying this by appropriate acts, rites, or ceremonies.
  Homage or reverence paid to a deity, esp. in a formal service.
  To adore a supernatural being or power.

- The *Collins English Gem Dictionary*:
  Reverence, adoration.

Three Unitarian ministers offered these definitions when addressing students who were in training for the ministry.

- Arthur Long:
  The aim of worship is trying to create a communal awareness of God. A recharging of spiritual batteries might also be one description.

- Sydney Knight:
  Worship is an experience felt within. In true worship, something more than words can convey is communicated.

13

- Frank Schulman:
  Worship is the human response to the awesome majesty of God's presence. Never, never trivialise worship, nor treat it as a joke. An act of worship is too serious for an ego trip.

- Finally, the Society of Friends:
  Worship is the response of the human spirit to the presence of the divine and eternal, to the God who first seeks us. The sense of wonder and awe of the finite creature before his creator cannot but lead to thanksgiving and adoration.

But ultimately we must each decide for ourselves what worshipping together means to us.

What features create an atmosphere for worshipping together?

We might learn something by considering just three traditions – Jewish, Catholic, and Protestant – and how their followers create a worshipping community.

A central feature of Jewish worship is the opening of the sacred Ark and the reading of the Torah from the hand-written Scrolls. The community repeats regularly the one great sentence, 'Hear, O Israel, the Lord our God, the Lord is one'. Synagogue worship includes a great sense of community, particularly at events such as a teenager's Bar Mitzvah, a wedding, or a funeral. The great festivals are precious to Jews and strengthen the sense of worshipping together: Passover, Shavuot, and Hanukkah, to name just a few. The community spirit starts in the home with a Sabbath meal and a blessing of the food; after the meal, the community spirit is equally evident in the synagogue. In addition, Jews have a deep sense of history and of their historic figures.

Catholic worship creates community worship through ritual, involving holy water, incense, bells, repetition, the use of rosary beads, the drama of the Mass, colour, works of art, the Stations of the Cross, the great Christian festivals, and the use of a missal. The believers revere the Virgin Mary and many saints. An image of the Pope appears in all the churches that I have visited. In parallel with the Jewish Bar Mitzvah, Catholics attribute great importance to a child's first communion, when whole families pack the church.

The Protestant church ranges from plain, almost Puritan communities to the high Anglican churches that have adapted many aspects of Catholicism; from the simplicity of some Scottish kirks (with no music at all, other than sung Psalms) and Quaker Meeting Houses (where a whole service can be held in silence) to Anglican churches with a great choral tradition. In general the Protestant tradition has emphasised the spoken word, especially the Bible, and (within the Anglican fold) the Apostles' Creed and the General Confession. To the spoken word it has added the sung word, through the use of hymns, which helped to teach its theology.

The Anglicans have their Book of Common Prayer. Unitarians have had their own 'prayer books': to name a few, *Orders of Worship* (published in 1932); *Every Nation Kneeling*, created by Will Hayes in 1954; *Services and Songs for the Celebration of Life*, created by Kenneth Patton, an American Universalist, in 1967; and Peter Godfrey's fine compilation of the Sheffield Orders of Worship (1976).

How can Unitarians create an atmosphere for worshipping together?

We must not throw out the baby with the bathwater! We must look at other traditions, recognise what is of value in them, and perhaps adapt them to meet our own needs.

Here are some of the factors that can contribute to communal worship: the building we meet in, and its aesthetics; music and silence; the spoken word, prayers and meditations, readings, hymns, and songs. Perhaps the greatest contributory factor for us is the people in the congregation themselves, their gifts and their needs. One important thing to note is that schoolchildren today only rarely sing hymns, and we now have the first or possibly second generation for whom hymn singing is unfamiliar; this could have an effect on our worship.

As I have said, the experience of worshipping together varies for each individual. I happen to love good music as part of congregational worship, but I have to be conscious that for others it might not be so. Some like long silences, whereas others are irritated by them. Some people want to hear an address each time, but others do not.

We should come to worship with sincerity, a sense of reverence (that doesn't exclude humour!), and sometimes with a sense of awe at our place in the community and in the universe. Revd Dudley Richards, a Unitarian minister now in his nineties, told me when I was eighteen years old, 'Peter, the church is a beloved community.' Over the years nothing has moved me from that view. If we are a beloved community, then we can worship together.

Background reading

Unfortunately, many of the Unitarian publications that have inspired me are now out of print, but here are some that I have found useful over many years.

Art and Religion by Von Ogden Vogt, Boston: Beacon Press, 1921.
    This has good chapters on art, music, architecture, and liturgy.
The Prayer Book Tradition in the Free Churches by A. E. Peaston,
    London: J. Clarke, 1965.
The Hymn Sandwich (a brief history of Unitarian worship) by
    Duncan McGuffie, 1982.
Handbook for Congregational Studies, edited by J.W. Caroll, C. S.
    Dudley, and W. McKinney, Nashville: Abingdon Press, 1986.

Handbook of Religious Services, Church of the Larger Fellowship, Boston: Skinner House Books, 1995.

Rejoice Together. Prayers, Meditations, and Other Readings for Family, Individual, and Small-Group Worship, edited by Helen R. Pickett, Boston: Skinner House Books, 1995.

Spirit of Time and Place, by Clifford Reed, London: Lindsey Press, 2002.

Meditation Manuals, various authors, various dates, published by Unitarian Universalist Association of America (www.uua.org/skinner/meditation.html).

Growing a Beloved Community (Twelve hallmarks of a healthy congregation), by Tom Owen-Towle, Boston: Skinner House Books, 2004.

The author

Revd Peter Hewis has held three very different ministries: in Bethnal Green for seven years, in Hinckley for 29 years, and as the Chaplain, Tutor, and Minister to the Unitarian congregation at Harris Manchester College in Oxford for five years. Among other interests, he has been a Liberal Councillor in Hinckley, and played the cornet in brass bands and the French horn in a military band. He is Secretary of the Ministers' Benevolent Society and a Trustee of the Send a Child to Hucklow Fund.

Questions for reflection and discussion

1. How do you define a worshipping community?

2. What are the essential elements of communal worship?

3. What do you receive from worship, and what do you contribute to it?

4. How might the experience of worship in your congregation be improved?

3 Empowering families: the congregation of all ages

Jim Robinson

Broadly speaking, the United Kingdom has become a secular country. Most young parents no longer consider it necessary or important to introduce their children to a community of worship. Children may still be christened, couples may still get married, and clergy still preside at funerals, but otherwise most British families consider church-going a poor use of their time. How can we swim against this current and attract families to Unitarian and Free Christian churches and chapels?

To put it simply, we need to listen to what young families want – and then create it. At Rosslyn Hill Unitarian Chapel, in north London, 46 children and teenagers are active members of our congregation. I asked them, and their parents, what they want from a Unitarian community. The seven teenagers who were gathered together that evening responded (in summary) as follows:

> We want to do activities that we cannot do anywhere else in our life. We want to get together in a group, without alcohol, and do things like group games, sleep-overs, movie nights, and special trips. We want to meet people we would not normally meet, like a psychic or a self-defence instructor, or a rock musician. We want to have adult leaders who enjoy us but don't rule over us. We want to belong to a chapel that is not like a school. We are proud to be Unitarian, because we can be who we are.

When I arrived at Rosslyn Hill Chapel, there had not been a teenager group for many years. Now we have 12 young people in this age group. Meeting together twice a month, they are empowered to create their own group, based on the model described above, with the guidance of a committed adult leader.

At a meeting of chapel parents I asked the same question: 'What do you want for your family at a Unitarian chapel or church?' The 14 gathered parents responded along the following lines:

We want a spiritual home which is inclusive and not exclusive. We have very busy lives, and want to come to church when we can, without guilt when we cannot. We want a children's programme that begins with a story in the chapel, so our children identify with this worship space. Then we want activities which teach them the same values that we are trying to teach them at home. We want them to see that it is not just their parents saying this is important, but a whole group of people also saying that values are important. We want our chapel to be child-friendly, and for adults to enjoy our children, even though children can be noisy sometimes. We want a place that we can come to as a family. Sunday morning is one of the few times when we are all together, without rushing somewhere. We want church to be relaxed and enjoyable. We want a safe crèche for the young ones, with the same adult every week. And we want a good sermon and service for the grown ups!

I also took the time to ask our chapel children what they wanted when they come to chapel. Here (in summary) is what a dozen children (aged 5 to 11) said:

We want to have fun. We want to be with our friends and make new friends. We want to do art projects. We don't want to take tests like at school. We like saying our affirmation every week ('We are the chapel of the open mind, the loving heart, and the helping hands'). We like lighting our candle every week and having circle time. We like our teacher, who is with us almost every week. We like having snacks.

Parents want their children to learn moral and spiritual values. The children want to have fun. If you can put together these two aims, then you can have a successful children's programme in your church or chapel.

Such a programme can take many forms. At the Broadway Avenue Unitarian Church in Bradford, there is a lively youth club. The youth club (Chalice Club) meets fortnightly, while the Sunday school (for children) meets every Sunday. They have used the Chalice Award scheme promoted by the General Assembly.[1] At the Old Chapel in Dukinfield, there is a regular Sunday School which meets at a separate time from the weekly service. They engage in activities that include arts and crafts, visits to places of interest, citizenship courses, and Unitarian heritage projects. Several times a year the children arrange special services in the chapel, and also an annual pantomime, which involves the entire congregation. Sponsorship is available for youth to attend weekend activities at the Nightingale Centre in Great Hucklow. Your Unitarian church, chapel, or Free Christian church can meet the needs of your families in its own unique way.

Surely, the larger society needs our presence and creativity. A study quoted on BBC Radio claimed that 95 per cent of British families with children under the age of 16 do not regularly attend any religious service. When I ask families in my neighbourhood the reason for their non-attendance, this is what I hear from them:

> *Religion is irrelevant. It doesn't help me to live my daily life. My family is busy, and Sunday is the one time when we can relax. Religion in the UK is out of date. It is stuck in the past.*

In order to attract some of these families, we must honestly seek to meet their needs. The worship services need to be relevant for the adults. They must help people in their real lives, and not consist merely of lectures or platitudes. We need to make Sunday morning family-friendly and relaxed. The activities must be fun for their children. Young families are missing a sense of community, and they do want a place where their values are reinforced by a larger group. We can attract families, but only by listening to what they truly want.

This will entail outreach. Members of your church and chapel need to speak with young families, not to recruit them, but to find out what they would want from a spiritual home. If young parents feel that you are truly listening to them, then there is a good chance they will become interested. The best way to attract families is the personal approach.

Of course, this means that we must ask the key question: do we really want children in our Unitarian congregation? However well behaved, children mean more noise and chaos. Some members may want to preserve a quieter Sunday morning atmosphere. Your congregation must come to an honest answer about the presence of children and youth. But even if you want to keep Sunday morning child-free, you can still create a children's chapel at another time of the week. The question is commitment: do you really want it to happen? Are you willing to budget the resources (financial and human) to create a vibrant spiritual home for young families?

The good news is this: a Unitarian or Free Christian church or chapel can be the kind of spiritual home that young families are looking for. The Unitarian message is inclusive and value-oriented – exactly what many parents are looking for. Children's chapel can be fun – just what the children are looking for. Teen programming can be empowering – just what teenagers are looking for. With work, we can attract and keep young families, and we can create spiritual communities that contain all age groups.

Note

1. S. Ashworth, S. Jones, S. Ramage, and S. Tinker, Unitarian
   Chalice Award: Leaders' Pack, Sheffield: GA Religious Education
   and Youth Department, 2001.

The author

In 1835 Jim Robinson's great-great-grandmother became a
Unitarian in Boston, Massachusetts, USA. Each generation
has continued the heritage, making Jim a fifth-generation
Unitarian. So when he decided to enter the ministry, there was
little question about the religion. Jim was ordained in 1978
into the Unitarian Universalist ministry and served churches
in Concord and Brewster, Massachusetts. His Brewster
congregation was given the Pickett Award, the highest
recognition given by the UUA for an individual congregation.
He became the settled minister at Rosslyn Hill Unitarian
Chapel, London, in May 2004.

Questions for reflection and discussion

1. If you currently have parents, children, and teenagers at
   your church or chapel, have you listened carefully to what
   they want? What might excite them enough to bring their
   friends along?

2. If you do not have families (or very few of them), do you
   have the energy to start a meaningful children's chapel and
   a teenagers' programme?

3. Would you be willing to hire someone to co-ordinate a
   children's chapel if there was nobody suitable in the
   congregation?

4 Being together – whatever our ages

Michael Dadson

How many people reading this chapter have recently logged on to check their e-mails, sent someone a video clip via their mobile phone, or switched on their i-pod to listen to their latest downloads? It's a 'brave new world', all right! And how strange the 'old world' would seem to today's young people, if they could go back to a time in Britain within living memory when *'there was no television; almost nobody had central heating – they used a coal fire with a back-boiler to heat their water, so a bath was rarely taken more than once a week; very few people had a telephone, even fewer owned a fridge, and the computer had not yet been invented'* (Ellis 2000).

While the current scale and pace of change might lead older voices to exclaim 'Stop the world; I want to get off!', a younger person might retort: 'You can keep *your* world; I'm glad I was never on it!' Lines are thus drawn, and loyalties established; generational groups are identified, gaps observed . . . and society fractures into separate pieces. 'Twas ever thus, you might say: you can't expect the older generation to keep pace with the young ones, or the younger generation to look back when they are busy surging ahead. A generation gap is inevitable – and we simply need to learn how to live with it.

Do we accept the 'generation gap'?

You can tell a culture is in trouble when its elders walk across the street to avoid meeting its youth.
(Wheatley 2002)

So wrote Margaret Wheatley, co-founder of The Berkana Institute, who develops radical new ideas for organising society and its component groups in chaotic times. If it is true that society in general tends to accept this separation of the generations, are we as Unitarians content to collude with it? Might we not have something to say about it, first within our own community and then more widely to our fellow citizens? Perhaps it should be emphasised that when a gap appears, and remains, between groups of people – groups of all kinds – it is because those people allow it to be so. Separation is the result of how we as human beings react to differentness; it is not the result of the differences themselves. The question is: do we settle for divisions rather than working to increase mutual understanding?

As Unitarians, we honour understanding and respect across social and cultural differences, so that they do not divide. Does it not then follow that, as Unitarians, we should honour and respect understanding across *generational* differences, so that they do not divide? In other words, surely good Unitarian practice will lead us to be able to overlook the 'generation gap' – perhaps even to live without any such thing in our community at all. Surely, in response to Margaret Wheatley's warning, we should assert that a culture is just as much 'in trouble' when the youth cross the street to avoid the elders – indeed when anyone crosses over to avoid anyone else (which reminds me of a tale, told long ago, about a Samaritan on a journey from Jerusalem to Jericho ...).

> Our natural state is to be together. Though we keep moving away from each other, we haven't lost the need to be in relationship. Everybody has a story, and everybody wants to tell their story in order to connect. If no-one listens, we tell it to ourselves, and then we go mad.
> (Wheatley 2002)

Naming the problem – a 'health warning'

Beware the condition known as 'stuckness'. Not only is it unhealthy in itself, but it can lead to the negative behaviour known as 'lumping'.

> Stuckness *n. A condition of chosen immobility; a sense of arrival at final destination; a voluntary end of journeying.*

'Stuckness' comes from the impulse to shun change and uncertainty; settling instead for comfort and constancy; doing, saying, and thinking things according to prevailing rules and conventions: 'This is the way we do it here' (= 'That's it; I've made up my mind; I know where I stand'). Have you ever caught yourself saying something along the following lines: 'There will never be a singer to touch Frank Sinatra / Freddie Mercury / Daniel Bedingfield' *(choose one – or substitute your own nomination)*; or 'You wouldn't have seen us dressed like *that* in my day'?

> To lump *v. To group other people, different from oneself, into closed categories; drawing conclusions about them and establishing a distance, gap, or divide.*

'Lumping' is a form of behaviour that easily follows on from stuckness. Anything that is different and uncomfortable – whether it is new or old – is pushed away. Once it is distanced, it can be criticised, caricatured, and demonised. ('Oh they're always changing their minds; you can't trust anything *they* say.' ... 'That's just not singing.' ... 'See what they're wearing; I wouldn't be surprised if there were drugs about.')

Recognition and response

Can we as Unitarians refrain from getting stuck in our own age groups, and lumping all others into a category called 'Them'?

Do we dare to open up to one another, and work actively for understanding between different age-groups – the kind of understanding that strengthens and enriches a community? I am issuing a direct challenge here, but Stephen Lingwood, a Birmingham Unitarian who has studied youth ministry at Boston University, might even call it a dire necessity:

> If we do something now that keeps things the way we like and comfortable, but that leads to the eventual decline of Unitarianism after we're gone, then we're not recognising our inter-generational responsibility.
> (Lingwood 2004)

If we add to that the recognition of our inter-generational possibilities, have we got an exciting and vital project on our hands? Is it not possible that for us the challenge of the so-called 'generation gap' is in fact an opportunity to demonstrate the power and sheer appropriateness of Unitarian behaviour in and for our times?

What is the project?

The issue of *GA Zette* published on April 7th during the Annual Meetings of the Unitarian General Assembly at Chester in 2005 carried an account by Helen Royall (Youth Adviser in the Western Union) of the Senior Youth Group's discussions on how it feels to be a young Unitarian:

> Perhaps the most disturbing thing that came up in the discussion was that adults very rarely communicated with young people – they were more likely to talk at them or completely ignore them.
> (Royall/Unitarian Youth, April 2005)

In a subsequent paper entitled 'All-Age Learning', Helen reflects on how easy it is for all of us to make assumptions about people, based solely on their age-group, before we even begin to talk with them – or we may even decide not to talk with them at all. She suggests a few starter principles to help to open up what she describes as 'the magic of communication':

- Everyone, whatever their age and experience, has their own story to tell.
- It is worth showing deep respect for every person.
- Everyone is doing the best they can with the resources that they have.

What happens then is real communication, and as you imagine everyone really communicating, really listening – whatever their age – you might notice something rather magical beginning ... which has implications for the whole community.
(Royall, July 2005)

What is the key element in such open and two-way communication? What is the core behaviour that will establish a mood of trust? What is it that can disarm all differences, and particularly in this context help us to build bridges across the 'generation gaps'? It may indeed bring healing to a community, it may indeed yield magic, but it is no great mystery: it is simply good listening.

But this means rather more than polite listening, or tolerant listening; it means rather more than young people stifling a yawn as Auntie Elsie starts yet again to reminisce about 'the days when ...'. And it means rather more than smiling indulgently when the young ones come back into the Sunday morning service to tell us what they've been doing. It means deliberately setting out to create opportunities to spend time together, simply to get to know each other as people – in situations like walking together, eating together, travelling together ... or even simply sitting together for no other reason than to be together.

As a spiritual community, dedicated explicitly to honouring the individual – of whatever age – on his or her personal journey, how may we claim to be honouring either the person or their journey if we don't actually know a great deal about either? And as a loving community, dedicated to nurturing and supporting the individual – of whatever age – along the way, how can we hope to demonstrate our love for each other if we don't listen to one another's stories?

This is something that we can each and all take up as our own task and challenge – to set out to listen to one another and learn from one another. Let's also realise and celebrate the fact that there are many skilled Unitarians who can support us, encourage us, and train us in this endeavour; who have the skills to teach better listening to us all, whatever our ages. For the sake of truly loving relationships today, and for the sake of a stronger community tomorrow, may we all resolve to give one another a 'right good listening to'!

> The work of mending the broken bonds across the generations is critically important. It is always surprising and satisfying to both adults and young people to be able to talk together—everyone is surprised by the intelligence and commitment of each other. And in those meaningful conversations, people of all ages discover new perspectives, new ideas, new friends.
> (Wheatley 2005)

Afterthought: 'Tale from a Riverbank'

At a certain spot along the River Avon, just a few years ago, a village festival was held in celebration of Mid-Summer. People of all ages gathered in the community meadow beside the river to enjoy the music and dancing, the food and drink, the stalls and the entertainment that had been put together. But the high point of the evening came with The Grand Launch! Everyone, whatever their age and handiness, had designed and built a small floating vessel; it didn't matter what shape or size or colour it was, how likely or unlikely it appeared – just as long as it was their own work. Each vessel had a candle mounted on it, and as the light began to wane, every candle was lit and all the vessels were launched. Such a variety there was – a real testimony to the range of human imagination – and they all behaved so differently once they got into the river! Some raced away, caught by a breeze or a current, while others circled around or got caught up now and then on roots or weeds. Before long, the river, along an ever-lengthening stretch and right across its width, was a moving carpet of flickering lights, each one representing an individual from the village, but all of them together representing the whole village.

As the tapestry drifted in the softening gloom, you couldn't tell which vessel was which, which vessel was whose; you couldn't tell which was long or short or large or small, and you couldn't match them with either the name or the age of their creators. They were all equally there, equally individual, equally part of the whole.

Sources and references

Ellis, A.H. (2000, reprinted 2001) *Living Through an Age of Change*, Sale Green: privately published

Lingwood, S. (October 2004) 'The Generation Gap', e-mail discussion group, futures@smartgroups.com (last checked by the author July 2005)

Royall, H. (April 2005) 'Views from the Senior Youth Programme', *GA Zette*, Chester.

Royall, H. (July 2005) 'All Age Learning', paper written at the request of this author

Wheatley, M.J. (2002) *Turning to One Another*, San Francisco: Berrett-Koehler

Wheatley, M.J. (2005) Correspondence with author, January 2005

The author

Michael Dadson is the minister of the Unitarian communities in Macclesfield and Newcastle under Lyme. As a curate in the Church of England, he set up a music and drama project for teenagers from three churches. After leaving the Church, Michael worked for a year in Dorset Social Services as a care manager for elderly people at home, while waiting to take up his place on a teacher-training course, which led to five years as a Religious Education Co-ordinator in a middle school.

Questions for reflection and discussion

1. Do you personally enjoy socialising with people outside your own age group, or do you always prefer the company of people of your own age?

2. In what ways might a Unitarian outlook on life be said to counteract the human tendency towards 'stuckness'?

3. Is it liberating or threatening for congregations of older people to be encouraged to try new things?

4. If a congregation were to produce a statement, or covenant, committing members to include people of all ages, give one or two examples of what it might say.

5 Universalism and dual religious allegiance

Feargus O'Connor

Be ours a religion which, like sunshine, goes everywhere; its temple, all space; its shrine, the good heart; its creed, all truth; its ritual, works of love; its profession of faith, divine living.
(Theodore Parker)

Throughout my ministry at Golders Green I have placed these words of Theodore Parker on the front page of our congregational newsletter, as a Universalist affirmation and declaration of faith. It is in this spirit and from that theological perspective that I write this chapter, which presents the values that characterise one Unitarian Universalist congregation in London and its efforts to witness to the vision that inspires its worship, its social ideals, and its religious outreach.

What, it may be asked, does 'Universalist' mean in this context? And is the word being used in a 'Humpty Dumpty' sense? (*'"When I use a word", Humpty Dumpty said in a rather scornful tone* [to Alice in Looking-glass Land], *"it means just what I choose it to mean – neither more nor less."'*) As some Unitarians seem averse to this use of the word 'Universalist', I invoke the authority not only of Revd Dr Arthur Long, doyen of contemporary British Unitarian Christian theologians, but also once again that of Humpty Dumpty himself, who was fond of using 'portmanteau' words. (*'"You see, it's like a portmanteau – there are two meanings packed up into one word."'*) In his book *Current Trends in British Unitarianism,* Arthur Long sanctions the use of the word to describe not only the Christian belief in universal salvation for all humanity, but also that strand of

Unitarian thought and belief which searches for wisdom and enlightenment not solely in the Judaeo-Christian tradition but in the entire worldwide religious heritage of humankind. That belief and outlook go back at least to the period of the Enlightenment; they were evident in the lives and writings of several prominent nineteenth-century Unitarian thinkers, and were characteristic of several of the Transcendentalists. Jenkin Lloyd Jones, the advanced Unitarian radical thinker and secretary of the 1893 World Parliament of Religions, dreamed of building *'a temple of universal religion dedicated to the enquiring spirit of progress, to the helpful service of love'.*

Such a significant, albeit minority, strain of Universalist Unitarianism was evident too in the twentieth century, perhaps most notably in the writing and teaching of Will Hayes (1890–1959), a British Unitarian minister who was inspired by the wisdom of many and diverse religious traditions. Hayes, whose writings were highly regarded by early members of the World Congress of Faiths and by many fellow Unitarians, argued that there were two kinds of Unitarian: the 'Unitarians of the United World' – the Universalists – and those in the majority, whom he termed 'Christocentric', who adhered to the liberal Christian tradition.

Is a truly Universalist community practicable (or even desirable)?

What are the characteristics of a truly Universalist congregation? It must surely embrace an inclusive Unitarianism which nurtures and values each and every one of us as the unique souls that we are. It is a congregation which recognises no dogmas and creeds imposed by the dead hand of past authority, and no dull conformity with beliefs and conventions (however venerable and comforting) which our conscience and reason cannot accept. It is one which unites our diverse strands and heartfelt individual ideals in a higher unity, which brings together all that is of abiding worth in our own tradition and the traditions of other faiths in a strong sense of common purpose: a liberal religious idealism which accepts and values all that is precious and true in our common worldwide spiritual heritage and discards all that is narrow, sectarian, and divisive. All that matters is the ceaseless search for truth, and all false and groundless beliefs should be decisively rejected.

Closed-minded sceptics and religious dogmatists alike often express disbelief that the bold ideal of Universalism can be translated into reality; but many Unitarian congregations, here and in the United States, prove that it can be realised, and indeed it can be seen to inspire their congregational life and worship. The question remains, however: how inclusive can such a congregation actually be? Can it really unite Universalist theists, liberal Christians, pan-religionists, religious humanists, Pantheists, religious feminists, Neo-Pagans and upholders of the ideals of the Unitarian Earth Spirit Network, and other defenders of what American Unitarian Universalists call the 'interdependent web of all existence of which we are a part'? Can it bind us together in a spirit of free religious fellowship and mutual respect, to expand our spiritual horizons to embrace what we perceive to be authentic and valuable in every religious tradition, East and West? That surely is the decisive test of how Universalist a congregation actually is.

One question may be legitimately asked of congregations of this kind: '*Can those who come to us from other faith traditions be accepted as full members and participate with integrity in the life and worship of the congregation?*' There is no easy answer to that, for it must surely depend on the nature of the previous 'faith' or religious allegiance in question. Many Unitarians are suspicious of the very word 'faith' and what it sometimes

33

stands for: as often appears to be the case with Evangelical Christian believers, it looks suspiciously like blind trust or being coerced into assenting to something that you suspect may not be true. Nor should it be forgotten that those of us not born into the Unitarian fold mostly come from some other tradition and we all, to a greater or lesser extent, bear the marks of our religious upbringing and the faith tradition from which we have come, even if it is merely a matter of reacting strongly against it.

Golders Green Unitarians: a case in point

In answering my own question, I look to our own congregation at Golders Green, and the diverse religious and humanist origins of our members and friends. (I should explain that we have two categories of membership: 'Full Members' and 'Friends', the latter choosing to give moral and financial support without being entitled to exercise full voting rights.) We have several members whose family origins are in the Brahmo Samaj; our previous secretary comes from a Hindu family; and our interfaith community co-ordinator is a practising Muslim who has been an active Friend and regular attender at GGU worship for several years.

We have Jewish, Muslim, Hindu, Buddhist, liberal Christian, and humanist Friends whose moral support and goodwill we value immensely. Several of these regularly attend our services and support our various social, humanitarian, and charitable activities. Two of our regular attenders are from an Iranian Muslim background. A practising Muslim from India was co-opted to serve on our management committee, comes to GGU most Sundays for worship, and actively supports our charitable and interfaith outreach work. Two practising Liberal Jewish Friends have loyally maintained their links with us for several years; another, Monty Miller, now sadly deceased, was very well known in Golders Green and in the pages of the *Jewish Chronicle* for his dual attendance at the local Reform synagogue and at GGU. Evidently Monty himself saw no conflict between being a committed but questioning Jew and a loyal and well-loved friend of our congregation, which he regarded as a community of open-minded fellow seekers after truth. All these attenders share a sense of gratitude that our congregation has a Universalist ethos which transcends any narrow and constraining 'Christian' perspective; they value the fact that we avoid paying lip service to the official General Assembly Object of 'upholding the liberal Christian tradition': a declaration which the vast majority of our members and friends could not in conscience make.

Unitarians and the Brahmo Samaj

We now come to the interesting case of the Brahmo Samaj, whose Universalist religious outlook and spiritual tradition of pure theism can be said to be close to Unitarianism. Indeed, the Brahmo Samaj has had close ties with our Unitarian movement since the time of its great founder, Rammohun Roy. At Golders Green we see no conflict between adherence to the Brahmo Samaj and membership of a Unitarian congregation like ours. In fact my personal experience over several years as minister of Golders Green Unitarians has convinced me that our committed Brahmo members are an integral and valued part of our GGU family. Two have served on our committee and played a full and active part in our congregational life for over 30 years, and I know that Brahmos always feel welcome at our services.

In 2004 I led two Brahmo Samaj memorial meetings in our church, conducted a traditional Brahmo funeral, and, preaching at the annual Maghotsav celebration at GGU on the Universalist message of Rammohun Roy, emphasised the close links that have united our two traditions since the time of

35

Mary Carpenter. Moreover, the Brahmo Samaj has always had an honoured place at our interfaith services; and our occasional celebrations of the life and spiritual legacy of Rabindranath Tagore, whose writings and spiritual wisdom have inspired me for many years, have become a popular fixture of our GGU congregational life. Yet, however spiritually close they are to Unitarians, Brahmos are certainly not in any sense 'Christian'. This raises the question of how far the clause in our General Assembly Object that commits us to 'the upholding of the liberal Christian tradition' serves to encourage or discourage inquirers from other religious traditions. Can they be made to feel truly at home in our Unitarian churches?

If the Brahmo Samaj can be accepted by Unitarians as a sister religious tradition, Universalist in essence like ours, what criteria should guide us in deciding how far other religions are compatible with modern Unitarianism and the spirit of our GA Object?

Is there a limit to Universalist tolerance?

Although some may argue that our Unitarian movement should be open to all religious currents, it is surely important to distinguish between welcoming all comers and having a syncretistic and uncritical approach to all religions. I would argue that no Unitarian congregation could accept into full membership fundamentalist religious believers who declared an allegiance to dogmas and creeds which claimed an exclusive revelation that was not open to reasoned examination and the scrutiny of our critical intelligence.

A real and serious conflict arises only when there is dogmatic adherence to a belief system which does not respect the liberal and rational values that we proclaim and try our best to live by. Herein surely lies the fundamental importance of the supplementary clause in our GA Object, which, in the spirit of Universalism, empowers the Assembly to affirm the liberal religious heritage and 'learn from the spiritual, cultural and intellectual insights of all humanity'. In the spirit of the Jewish sage Maimonides, we should 'seek the truth from every source'.

GGU may be taken as an example of a London congregation inspired by such an ideal: we try to rise to the challenge of making all comers welcome at our services and our many social, charitable, and outreach activities. Like other Unitarian congregations, we make every effort to be truly sensitive to the diverse needs of our multicultural society: in the past year we have had evenings of Iranian classical poetry, Irish harp music, multilingual poetry readings featuring Arabic, Hebrew, and Urdu poets reading their original works, and several Bengali events with Indian classical music. We have hosted discussions and debates between Muslims and Hindus, and encounters between Jewish and Palestinian peace activists. Having friendly relations with the local Jewish community, we have many Jewish visitors and, like some UUA congregations, we would warmly welcome more Jewish Unitarians ('Jewnitarians') and happily integrate them into our congregation. Because there is no adherence on our part to 'upholding the liberal Christian tradition', Jewish friends and visitors feel that there is no psychological barrier to their full acceptance of our Universalist ethos.

Is it not in this spirit that, in our worship and outreach, Unitarian congregations can be true to the General Assembly's commitment to 'learn from the spiritual, cultural and intellectual insights of all humanity', and be true too to the Universalist values of wisdom and compassion embodied in the great religions and the world's literary heritage, which should inspire us in all works and deeds?

Sources and references

Boeke, Richard (2002) 'Ugly duckling or swan? Is Unitarianism a universal religion?', *Prospects for the Unitarian Movement,* edited by Matthew F. Smith, London: The Lindsey Press

Chryssides, George (1998) *The Elements of Unitarianism,* Shaftesbury, Dorset: Element Books

Hayes, Will (2004) 'My country, my church, my religion', reprinted in *Journal of the Unitarian Ministry*

Long, Arthur (1997) *Current Trends in British Unitarianism,* Belfast: Ulster Unitarian Christian Association

Marshall, Vernon (1999) 'Unitarians and other religions', *Unitarian Perspectives on Contemporary Religious Thought,* edited by George D. Chryssides, London: The Lindsey Press

Marshall, Vernon (2004) 'Dual loyalties: Unitarianism and Neo-Paganism', *Journal of the Unitarian Ministry*

O'Connor, Feargus (2004) 'The World Congress of Faiths and Unitarianism', *Journal of the Unitarian Ministry*

Usher, Andrew (editor) (2003) *Golders Green Unitarians: Centenary Voices,* London: Golders Green Unitarians

The author

A confirmed 'Quakertarian', Revd Feargus O'Connor has been passionately concerned for all of his adult life about peace and global justice. Long active in animal-welfare causes, he led the first-ever interfaith animal celebration in Britain. He is secretary of the World Congress of Faiths, with a particular interest in promoting dialogue with enlightened humanists, Quakers, and other liberals to counter the effects of fundamentalism. He is currently engaged in postgraduate studies concerning religious and philosophical beliefs about life after death. He has been minister of Golders Green Unitarians since 2001.

Questions for reflection and discussion

1. Can we be committed Unitarians and still retain previous religious allegiances?

2. Does Unitarianism sometimes encourage an uncritical acceptance of religious differences – and if so, what might be the consequences of that?

3. What should a Unitarian congregation be prepared to do to embrace the insights found in other traditions of thought?

4. Do we need to change our use of meditation, prayer, and hymns to take account of the diverse temperaments and spiritual needs of newcomers from non-Christian religious backgrounds?

6 Good local governance and congregational dynamics

John Clifford

In this chapter I use the term 'Unitarian' to denote the congregations of our General Assembly, but of course many of them go back some 350 years, while the word 'Unitarian' has been in use in English for only the past 230 years. The result is that our varied origins are sometimes reflected in other names on our notice boards and in trust deeds: for example, *Free Christian, [English] Presbyterian, [General] Baptist,* and *Universalist.*

I will not deal directly with the different polity (organisational structure) in the Non-Subscribing Presbyterian Church in Ireland, but many of the general points made here are applicable to that context.

The concept of governance

'Governance' refers to the *way* in which decisions are made and implemented, rather than the actual decisions taken. Our governance has been shaped not only by our religious/theological history, but by the legal framework of charity and trust law in both Scotland and England & Wales. Unitarians (and others) have struggled with limited success to incorporate many reforms enacted in the last 20 years, and already the British government and the Scottish Executive have plans to introduce further legislation, mentioned below.

Some maintain that a church is a unique, spiritual form of community, to which neither legal nor business forms are appropriate. I maintain that our spiritual communities are not monastic orders, nor private clubs. Our spiritual communities exist to provide our larger society with models and practical interventions, and our members with caring support. Our defining activity – public worship – is usually referred to as our 'service'. We deal with practical issues of temporal power, in addition to personal relationships and devotional practices. We have goals/ objects/ purposes. We need to make judgements about how well we are fulfilling these, even when they are difficult to quantify. We need to see connections between our values and our efforts to live them out in a social context. We need to act responsibly towards those whom we call to leadership. For all these reasons, governance issues are important.

Unitarian governance in practice

The local congregation, being a face-to-face community, is the basic unit in our structure. Our congregations are 'autonomous': that is, important decisions affecting the life of a congregation are made by its members. Central pillars of our tradition are democratic procedures and 'Open Trusts', i.e. objects that do not require adherence to any formal statement of beliefs by members or ministers. Officers (including the 'minister') are elected by members and are accountable to members.

Most of our congregations have buildings. As our congregations are voluntary associations rather than companies, they have no legal *persona*, so formal title to property is held in trust by trustees for the benefit of the congregation. These trustees will be (or they were originally) local people of standing connected with the congregation. Over time, funds may have been established to assist with the expenses of the building(s); these, particularly stock-market investments, may also be held by the same trustees. Sometimes our trustees appoint their own successors; sometimes the congregation makes the appointments. This should be specified in the document that originally set up the trust – the trust deed – which ideally should also specify particular regulations for the decision-making process of the trustees: how often they should meet, what powers of decision they have, etc. If trustees appoint their successors, it is possible for this body to grow remote from the congregation that it exists to serve.

- If your congregation has a building, do you know where your trust deed is kept, and what it says?
- Do incoming trustees receive a copy of the deed before assuming trusteeship?
- Do officers of the congregation (including the minister or appointed lay leader) have access to a copy?
- Is an annual report, including a financial report and accounts, prepared? Is a copy sent to the secretary of the congregation?

Each of our congregations should have a 'governing document' – a constitution – which sets out the rules and procedures for making decisions. Another way of saying this is that the constitution governs the distribution and application of power. Any 'management committee' elected to run the programme of the congregation will in fact be the trustees of the congregation, and they hold their power in trust, just as the building trustees hold the title to the building in trust.

- Do elected members of the committee have a copy of the constitution?
- Do ordinary members of the congregation get a copy of the constitution when they join?
- Is there a reference copy easily available to members and friends and visitors?
- Is there a clear process for deciding who is a member and who is not?

Member organisations should hold an annual meeting to receive reports from the officers, discuss any forward plans, and conduct elections as required by the constitution.

- Does your annual report quote the purpose/ object of the congregation from the constitution, so that the annual meeting can judge how well the congregation has met its responsibilities during the year, and decide what changes or developments need to be planned for the coming year?
- Do the annual financial report and accounts give clear information about sources and amounts of income, and categories and sums of expenditure?
- Are the accounts reviewed by someone independent of the committee (or, at least, independent of the treasurer)?
- Does the treasurer present a draft budget for forward planning?
- Are all papers received by participants in plenty of time to read them beforehand?

The greater the number of positive answers you can give to these questions, the better.

In Unitarian congregations, members covenant (agree) with each other to give caring support in the struggle to find meaning in life and to live this meaning. Membership does not require conformity to a set of beliefs (i.e. a creed), but it entails a commitment to being part of a religious community and sharing in our religious quest in this community. The most common definition of membership in our congregations is that someone has signed the membership book and made a financial contribution of record (usually a nominal sum) to indicate his or her general assent to the object(s) of the congregation. Thus it is loyalty that holds us together, rather than shared beliefs. Common identity is sustained in face-to-face interactions and expressed in terms of commitment to the use of reason, to tolerance of others' opinions, and to the widest

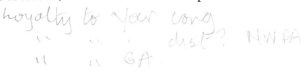

definition of human freedom that the group can sustain. Loyalty depends on trust, and good governance can foster and nurture trust through a framework that promotes openness, the involvement of members in discussions of important issues, and the setting of boundaries to guard against the risk of manipulation.

Good governance will not guarantee good decisions. Bad governance, however, can frustrate well-intentioned folk and allow chaos, even corruption, to dominate. Lack of open procedures allows manipulation by a few strong personalities – who may well be honest and well intentioned, but nevertheless can cripple or distort the spiritual and practical development of the congregation.

An example of good governance

Congregation X has about 25 'active' members, with an average Sunday attendance of 13. The age profile is slightly better than many of our congregations, but still there are few regulars under the age of 40, and many are over 60. The church building easily seats 150, and typically one or two people sit on each 8-seater pew (starting, of course, with the pews farthest from the pulpit!). The committee (of eight members plus attending minister) meets about every six weeks. The chairperson has a friendly, business-like style and keeps discussion focused on the agenda items, so meetings take between 90 minutes and two hours.

The treasurer does an excellent job in preparing the accounts and making reports to the committee, but had not realised that preparing a budget for the coming year was an important part of the job. With a bit of help, a forward budget is prepared. Preparation of the item on expected building-repair expenditure leads to the resurrection of a report on the state of the building from two years previously, which had been set to one side. This prompts the committee to seek professional advice on urgent and non-urgent expenditure; on the implications of having a listed building; and on insurance matters. Additionally, the committee lists for itself the main options for the future, and obtains professional advice on possible marketing of the building; potential joint-use options; and possible grants to bring the building into a safe and perhaps a more user-friendly state.

Committee members are allocated specific responsibilities for making contacts and getting information. Papers are prepared and circulated within the committee. A short congregational meeting is called to inform members of the issues that the committee is facing, and its efforts to obtain the best information possible. Meantime, a working party examines the trust deed to determine the responsibilities of trustees. Trustee status is clarified, and consideration is given to the need to appoint new trustees. Next the constitution is examined. This shows that the committee needs to take definite steps to clarify who is and who is not a member. This is done.

Arrangements for an extraordinary general meeting are made. They include visits to homebound members to explain the issues and provide a means for them to express their opinions to the forthcoming EGM; circulation to every voting member of reports for each of the options explored by the committee; circulation of a decision tree for the EGM to give the committee guidance on the direction that the congregation feels most comfortable to explore; reassurance to members that their opinions count, and that no irrevocable action will be taken without their further authority. Note especially:

- Everybody feels empowered in this decision process. Although some are very keenly disappointed by the actual decision, no one feels left out of the process, and all discussions have taken place within an atmosphere of care

and inclusiveness, and with a feeling that the best information available has been presented.
- Loyalty and group identity have been affirmed; the congregation and its committee are at the beginning of what could well be a long process, likely to take years, not months, and there is a high degree of trust. Members know what the issues are, and they understand the basis on which further decisions will be made.

Future legislation that may affect church governance

Space does not permit a detailed scrutiny of the legal context in which church communities operate. But it may be helpful here to list certain proposals by the government which may be relevant to church governance.

- Central government is proposing to bring ministers of religion within employment-protection provisions. The exact provisions for this are still under discussion, but they will undoubtedly affect the dynamics of the relationship between ministers and their congregations.
- The government is proposing a new form of charity organisation: a 'Charitable Incorporated Organisation (CIO)', adoption of which will at first be voluntary but may eventually become mandatory. The intention is to make charity governance more transparent, and comparisons between various charities easier.
- Tax benefits for registered charities are based on a concept of 'public benefit', and the government is considering enacting legislation to the effect that public worship in England and Wales is presumed to be a public benefit. This statutory presumption may be challenged by secular organisations; we need to be clear what real benefit we do offer the public in return for tax benefits on our income.

- The government and the Charity Commission for England and Wales are considering the question of payment of trustees. Any relaxation of the current negative presumption of payment would enable ministers to be full members of the management committee. Is this desirable?
- At present chapels/churches registered under the Registration of Places of Worship Act (1852) are not required to register under the Charities Acts, even though they may represent substantial financial assets held for the benefit of the congregation. This may change in the foreseeable future.

Sources and suggestions for further reading

Beasley-Murray, Paul (1998) *Power For God's Sake*, Carlisle: Paternoster Press. (The final chapter was the basis of the Essex Hall Lecture for 1999.)

Bolam, C. Gordon and others (1968) *The English Presbyterians, from Elizabethan Puritanism to Modern Unitarianism*, Aberdeen: George Allen and Unwin. (For those who are interested in the historical factors that brought our various strands together, and the impact that they had on each other.)

Charity Commission for England and Wales (July 2004) 'Guidance for Charities: How To Be An Effective Trustee', www.charitycommission.gov.uk/supportingcharities/ efftrustintro.asp (last checked February 2005). (The best single source for high-quality free advice on charity governance.)

Charity Commission for England and Wales (January 2005) 'Publications – Detailed List', www.charitycommission.gov.uk/publications/ccpubs2.asp (last checked February 2005). (Contains the text of CC publications, many in Welsh as well as English.)

Commission on Appraisal, Unitarian Universalist Association
(1997) *Interdependence, Renewing Congregational Polity*, Canada: Unitarian Universalist Association. (A very thoughtful and detailed consideration of congregational governance issues in the North American context. Lots of lessons for British Unitarians.)

Her Majesty's Government (2004) 'Charity Reform', www.homeoffice.gov.uk/comrace/active/charitylaw/index.html (last checked February 2005). (For the latest information about government intentions as new charity legislation is steered through Parliament.)

Hind, Andrew (1995) *The Governance and Management of Charities*, High Barnet: Voluntary Sector Press. (A detailed account of governance issues for charities, translating insights from company governance to the voluntary sector. Most models are based on organisations larger than our congregations, but the underlying analysis is helpful.)

Wesley, Alice B. (2001) *The Minns Lectures of 2000–2001*, to be found at 'Other UU History Resources', www.uua.org/uuhs/ UUresources/UUresources.html#minns (last checked November 2004). (With reference to our 'sister' congregations in the United States, the author argues that congregational autonomy was never intended to mean isolation, and that the slide from autonomy to isolation over the generations has blunted the effectiveness of the church's service and blurred the outlines of the model for society.)

The author

Revd John Clifford came into our liberal religious community via Universalism during his student days in the United States at the time of the merger of Universalists and Unitarians there. He is currently the Executive Secretary of the International Council of Unitarians and Universalists and was for 12 years the Deputy General Secretary of the General Assembly. He has served as a minister with Unitarian congregations in England, Scotland, and Wales and had pastoral oversight of a largely American congregation in Germany when he served in the Secretariat of the International Association for Religious Freedom. He has a certificate in charity management from South Bank University.

Questions for reflection and discussion

1. What is the worst example of governance practice that you have encountered in a Unitarian congregation? (The author knows of the case of a Treasurer who gave excuses rather than financial reports to seven consecutive monthly meetings, and a Committee and full-time minister who allowed this to continue.) What practical steps could be taken to remedy the situation that you have raised?

2. What is the impact on any group in which the decision makers do not take responsibility for the organisation's financial health, or for ensuring that decisions taken are actually implemented?

3. The author offers the following list of value-based perspectives as typical of what most British Unitarians would support: (a) that everyone is entitled to be treated with respect and fairness; (b) that relationships based on mutual caring are our most meaningful and transforming encounters with God; (c) that the ministry of the church to the world is the job of the whole church; (d) that we are part of the natural world, and responsible for our impact on it; (e) that the church's message to our divided and troubled world is a call for justice and healing; (f) that reason is an essential tool for understanding. Can you make your own list and then try to connect each value to a governance issue?

7 Dealing with congregational conflict

Margaret Hamer

I write this chapter from the standpoint of a private individual, as someone with no training in conflict resolution, but the experience of having observed serious conflict or division of opinion in every Unitarian congregation to which I have belonged. Since I was never one of the leading protagonists involved, I am left asking the questions: *Why are Unitarians so prone to conflict? Why is religious conflict so particularly bitter? How do we deal with it? How might this be improved?* You will note that I do not consider the topic *How can it be avoided altogether?* I am a realist. Moreover, serious disagreement, if well handled, can sometimes have some productive outcomes.

Unitarianism, which claims to be 'the church of the open mind', rejects the imposition of any creed. The same resistance to authority in matters theological seems to extend to our attitude to church governance in general. Most congregations cherish their autonomy and resist any move towards centralisation. Our 'go it alone' mentality, taken to extremes, can result in church closure. Yet we bewail our declining number of members, even as we promote the relevance of our spiritual outlook to a needy world. Viewing ourselves in the mirror, we have to admit that we are more prone to conflict than other religious groups, we have fewer resources to deal with it, and we have less agreement about the means to resolve it. Self-discipline is not one of our strengths; lack of it is contributing to our decline.

Whenever a serious dispute occurs in a congregation, it is inevitable that the leader will become involved, no matter how distant s/he was from the original cause. Leaders are the suns around which we lesser planets revolve. A leader is the focus of our collective attention. Next to God, we want leaders on our side – unless, of course, our quarrel is with them. Church disputes are often characterised by the bitterness of their in-fighting and the aftermath of damage that they leave behind. (A Welsh chapel – not Unitarian – that I once knew was locally known as 'Chapel Spite': a title that says it all.) Nasty deeds can be performed under the cloak of piety.

Tensions: destructive or creative?

All Unitarian congregations exist in a state of real or potential tension. Factors that account for this include differing religious viewpoints; differing interpretations of the leadership role; different generational needs (most of us are senior citizens, but we wish to attract young families); anxiety over church finances; casual practice over membership; over-reliance on a small band of volunteers to run each church (and then accusing them of being a clique); the need for change – and the resistance to it; and the ever-present pull between the assertive individual will and the collective good of the community. This list does not pretend to be exhaustive, but it will, I suspect, be familiar to most Unitarians.

Tension can be either positive or negative. It can lead to creative outcomes; it can open up honest exchanges of view, and lead to the exploration of differing solutions; it can help to clarify issues, challenge complacencies, and flush out hidden agendas. But only if it is addressed with care and responsibility. Without agreed procedures, and in the absence of mutual respect, it can explode into self-righteous recrimination and underhand politicking. When this happens, everyone loses: the individual, the congregation, and the greater movement.

One period ripe for potential trouble comes after the honeymoon that follows the appointment of a new leader. Old allegiances may still be strong, and the newcomer may be seen by some as a usurper. The longer the previous ministry and the more loved the incumbent, the more a substantial period of mourning is essential as people adjust to the vacancy. Either an experienced interim minister or an extended period of self-management is strongly advisable, to allow a congregation to start making realistic plans for the future. Simply planting a new rose in the gap left by an old one is bad gardening; criticising a new leader for not being his or her predecessor is equally bad practice. Every probationary leader should be given training in conflict management.

Resolving conflict: some ground-rules

When a church committee is in serious dispute with its leader, this should never be allowed to develop into a situation where personal attacks take the place of debate about the issues, and the many are seen to turn upon the one. The religious leader occupies an oddly isolated position, one which has largely escaped the regulating procedures of other professions. However seemingly compromising the evidence against an individual may be, justice demands that a friend/advocate should accompany the leader concerned, both to speak on that person's behalf and to see fair play. It is also essential that leaders are given clear job specifications, subject to regular review and altered when necessary, so that annual performance can be measured against an agreed yardstick. All too often, expectations are left unspecified – and the result is mutual recrimination.

I have compiled the following list of suggestions for handling congregational conflict from various sources, some Unitarian, some not.

- Face the conflict: identify it and define the area of disagreement.
- Focus on issues, not personalities.
- Try to view differences of opinion as helpful, not threatening. Through exploring them, the best course of action will become available.
- Agree on some civilised methods of debate: for example, we will not interrupt one another (unless invited); we will choose a Chair who will not be involved in the debate and through whom all remarks will be addressed; we will try to agree an agenda.
- Record what is said, and produce a transcript if possible.
- Assume that resolution of the conflict will take more than one meeting.
- Accept that, if the dispute is a matter of conscience, the best possible outcome is an uneasy peace.
- Listen attentively to what is said, and be prepared to modify your position.
- Recognise mutual need in a congregation. Age needs the energy of youth; youth needs the time and input of age.
- Adapt to changing times. Victorian practice doesn't fit the needs of the twenty-first century.
- Consider the possible effects of change before implementing it.
- Empower all the parties in a conflict. All should be part of the resolution.
- Aim for consensus, rather than voting or yielding simply in order to keep the peace.
- When all attempts at internal reconciliation fail, consider engaging a professional mediator as a final resort. This should be agreed by all parties.

Finally, whenever a new church committee is appointed, provide all members and leaders with copies of the church constitution and the Guidelines for Ministers and Congregations, issued by Essex Hall. At present these exist as three separate documents, of which 'Guidelines III: A Code of Practice for Congregations and their Leaders, April 2000', deals specifically with conflict resolution. (The Guidelines are presently undergoing revision and will eventually appear as a single document.) This resource advises the best practice to be followed in all aspects of church life. Its limitation is that the guidelines lack the force of law and exist solely as recommendations. A congregation may consult them and choose to disregard their counsel. The resulting free-for-all confrontation diminishes the credibility of Unitarianism nationally.

Using a mediator

Whichever way of handling a dispute is chosen, it must have the support of all the parties involved. It is essential that the authority of the process is generally accepted. For once, dissent should be silent. When conflicts between congregations and their leaders cannot be resolved at the local level, recourse can be made to any one of several agencies: either the Ministerial Fellowship or the Unitarian Association of Lay Leaders; the General Secretary at Essex Hall; and the Review and Support Panel of the General Assembly. The latter consists of three volunteers who have considerable experience in handling congregational disputes. Their voluntary status places some limits on their usefulness, in that they may have difficulty in setting up meetings at short notice; they may be called on by several congregations more or less simultaneously; and they are often invited in too late, when the battle has already been fought and irreparable damage done.

Compromise, co-operation, and reconciliation are not, alas, words that invariably spring to mind when dealing with

Unitarians. However, such terms have a long and honourable tradition in the history of the sect that is closest to us theologically: the Society of Friends. (Unitarians have been described as 'Quakers with hymns'.) We can learn much from *Quaker Faith and Practice*, their book of Christian discipline, particularly Section Ten ('Our Community, Conflict within the Meeting, Individual Commitment') and Section Eleven (on all aspects of Membership, including the termination of individual membership when all attempts at unity have failed). Entry 4.21 on 'Disputes among Friends' reads:

> Monthly Meetings are recommended to appoint a group of experienced and knowledgeable Friends who would be available to give general assistance in the amicable settlement of disputes. If help from outside the Monthly Meeting is needed, enquiry should be made of the Clerk of the Meeting for Sufferings, who may suggest Friends qualified to give it. Techniques of problem-solving, mediation, counselling or meetings for clearness may be appropriate in particular instances where disputants wish to mitigate the consequences of confrontation.

It should be borne in mind that Friends were among the pioneers of conflict resolution as a distinct activity, and they have constantly sought reconciliation in the wider world. Presenting a case before an external Quaker mediator was a productive and educative experience in the case of one congregational conflict that I know of. Individuals felt obliged to make their case both reasonably and courteously before an impartial presence, which had not been the case previously. They were given the opportunity to reflect on their conduct, to listen attentively to the case for the opposition, and to put their arguments in a more open and detached way. Eventually the dispute was resolved. All the participants were unanimous in their praise of the outside facilitator.

If all else fails ...

If all attempts at reaching a solution fail and a breach ensues, the best outcome available may lie either in establishing a new fellowship or in transferring membership to another Unitarian congregation. This will often involve abandoning a much-loved building – always a painful course, but it is the people, not the settings, that constitute a living church. The lack of a building can bring certain advantages. It allows for fluidity in hiring locations, and flexibility in the style of services, although there may be problems in finding space for children's activities. It also avoids the sometimes crippling costs involved in maintaining a substantial place of worship.

Making a fresh start can stimulate the creative energies that are drained by conflicts. There may be no money to speak of initially, but this fact may oblige members to take a more realistic attitude to live giving; as a movement we are rather too inclined to exist parasitically on past legacies. There is no excuse for any member of a small, vibrant congregation to plead ignorance of the balance sheet. What does a meal in a restaurant cost? Or a ticket to a football match?

We are all flawed and imperfect beings, and we need to accept ourselves for what we are. When we look at others, particularly when we disagree with them, we often focus on their weaknesses and deficiencies and blame them for falling short of the standards that we demand of them. A healthy congregation is a community of mutual empowerment. Reason, tolerance, and respect for the freedom of others should begin at home.

Sources

Beasley-Murray, Paul (1998) *Power for God's Sake*, Carlisle: Paternoster Press.

Quaker Faith and Practice (1999) London: The Yearly Meeting of the
Society of Friends.

Unitarian General Assembly (2000) 'Guidelines III: A Code of
Practice for Congregations and their Leaders', London: Essex Hall.

The author

Margaret Hamer studied English Literature at university and
has taught and lectured in schools, colleges, and universities
in England, Denmark, Canada, and the USA, where she
encountered her first Unitarian congregation. After ten active
years in the Southampton church, she moved to East Anglia,
where she is now Chair of the Bury St Edmunds congregation.
She has been a columnist on *The Inquirer* and continues to be
active as editor of the newsletter of the Unitarian Women's
Group, and in matters concerning Religious Education. She
looks forward to a time of more open governance in
Unitarianism at the national level.

Questions for reflection and discussion

1. Conflicts, initially, are simply problems to solve. How does
   your congregation set about handling problems creatively?
2. Looking back on a problem that grew into a major conflict,
   how, with hindsight, would you have handled it differently?
3. In what ways might a relaxed policy over membership
   contribute to future problems in a congregation?
4. Should all congregational leaders receive on-going training
   in conflict resolution, or should this be the responsibility of
   the Chair? Would the services of a trained trouble-shooter
   (not necessarily Unitarian) be advantageous for each district?
5. How well do you know the 'Guidelines for Congregations'?
   Which would you choose to revise in the light of your
   experience?

8 Social activities and congregational well-being
Malcolm Sadler

In 1959, when my parents and I first visited Warwick Chapel after the Minister, Revd Harry Maguire, had invited me to serve as the organist there, we were somewhat shocked to find a shabby, neglected eighteenth-century chapel with Victorian additions, hardly any heating, and just five dim light bulbs. It was not an auspicious start, to say the least, particularly when Mrs Maguire said to us as we went in, 'Sit here, I've dusted this pew'! Compounding this sad state of affairs was the habit of the congregation, such as it was, to leave the building immediately after the service, barely allowing themselves time to shake the hand of Harry Maguire on the way out. And that was it: worship done for the week, and the building could be shut up until the following Sunday.

Unfortunately, this is still the case with too many of our churches and chapels today. They seem not to have realised that this is the twenty-first century, and people's expectations are much higher than they were 40 or 50 years ago. They want (if they want to belong to a religious community at all) to have churches that are warm, inviting, clean, and friendly, with something going on in addition to worship on Sundays.

I had come from a church with a strong social programme, and I found the complete absence of such a programme very frustrating in my new spiritual home. What was particularly disappointing was the lack of any opportunities for members and visitors (if any) to get together after the service to chat to each other. After some months, one of the members at Warwick, who had moved into a flat belonging to the chapel changing environment – an environment that is shaped at least as much by changing attitudes as it is by local demographics, or changes to traffic management and local parking arrangements. We also need to be mindful of the historical perspective that gives our movement its distinctive religious legacy of free thought and non-hierarchical church governance. Our study requires of us that we probe the true purposes of a congregation. Is worship its pre-eminent *raison d'être*, or do mutual support and service to the wider community have an equal, or greater, claim?

We should beware being satisfied with a single, narrow concept of what it means to be a congregation – except perhaps for legalistic, constitutional purposes. For example, the National Unitarian Fellowship (NUF) has pioneered innovative forms of religious fellowship that enable those who may live many hundreds of miles apart to get to know one another, and even to feel the bonds of religious community. The potential for remote interaction has been boosted immeasurably by the advent of the Internet – challenging still further our conventional notions of what religious community can be.

Although religious belief is not a primary theme of this book, the diversity of the authors can be seen to a degree in clear differences of theological outlook. As editor, I make no attempt here to try to resolve any such differences. However, readers will have to judge for themselves whether the underlying unity that Unitarianism advocates can be affirmed through the various chapters, or whether the divisions of opinion that exist might be such as to hinder the building of community both locally and nationally – when that should be so much a part of what the movement is about.

Readers are warned not to expect anything approaching a uniformity of style or pitch from such a free-thinking bunch of contributors as Unitarians are known to be. You will find that academic and analytical contributions sit here alongside unashamedly subjective offerings in which the writers draw primarily on personal history, rather than necessarily claiming any theoretical knowledge of, for example, the dynamics of church growth. None of the styles of writing that are evident here is presumed by the editor to be any more valid than any other. On the contrary, it is hoped that some surprising harmonies may be heard, although the melodies of the contributors are so distinctive and different.

In recognising that every chapel community is a meeting of unique souls, each with its own priorities and passions, we cannot rule out the possibility of conflict. Unitarian congregations may, in fact, be more prone to conflict than most mainstream churches, because we are not bound by a common creed (although it is difficult to know how this hypothesis might be scientifically proven one way or the other). Congregations upholding the Unitarian principle of free thinking in religious matters are undeniably vulnerable to damaging splits, because disagreements will rarely be overcome simply through deference to supposed religious authority in any form. Could it be that there is perhaps an increasing recognition that the movement needs to train more ministers and lay people to employ appropriate techniques of conflict resolution, and to understand group dynamics generally?

Ultimately, however, though we may be all too aware of the denominational weaknesses – not to mention our personal failings – that inhibit Unitarianism from rapidly becoming the major force for good that we believe it should be, many of us are sustained by a conviction that both the tide of history and everyday experience continually confirm that the liberating principles on which our liberal religious faith is founded are riches to be treasured.

As religious liberals, we Unitarians are increasingly seeking to define common values that can unite us – while maintaining our absolute rejection of fixed theological creeds as a test of religious fellowship. The revised Object of the General just next door, invited my parents and me into her sitting room after the service for a cup of coffee before we went home. It did not take long for the rest of the group to find this out, so it was then arranged that this lady would take a tray of coffee round into the vestry for everyone. From those small beginnings grew the regular brewing up of tea and coffee after each service, with a plate of biscuits, so that we could all have a chat together. It proved to be a most advantageous development, and it carries on to this day, except that these days we sometimes have homemade cake as well.

A religion based on relationships

In some church communities one can attend services for years and not know anything much about one's fellow worshippers. It does nothing for the well-being of the group. The mere fact of staying behind for 20 minutes or so encourages people to chat and to get to know one another better (and maybe to criticise the sermon).

As I am constantly saying in my sermons, relationships are what our religion is all about: relationships with those who worship with us, relationships with those of our wider circle whom we meet every day, and relationships with our God, by whatever name we choose to call Him/Her/It. So anything that we can do which encourages us to seek out and enjoy each other's company in a social sense is just as valuable as the hour spent in congregational worship each week.

At Warwick I felt that we should also have some form of social gathering on a weekday, say once a month, when we could have more time in which to get to know one another better. As the chapel was the only place we had, the obvious thing was to meet in members' homes for a small-scale social programme, and this we did for a good many years. It proved to be a most valuable part of chapel life, particularly after the early death of Harry Maguire, when we were without a minister for some considerable time: these social evenings helped to hold the group together.

Social events don't have to be grand, pretentious affairs: just a convivial chat over a cup of tea can work wonders, and if a bit of entertainment can be included, so much the better. It takes very little effort to get people to bring along a favourite CD, play a track, and explain why they chose it, in a sort of 'Desert Island Discs' evening. You can be a little bolder and have a general discussion, if only to plan a programme for the rest of the year. All you need is someone who is willing to act as host on a particular evening (or afternoon if, as in Warwick, you have a predominantly elderly, retired membership). There is much to be said for meeting on weekday afternoons where possible, because many older folk do not like going out at night, particularly in the winter. Plan things to suit your own situation, and take note of members' ideas and wishes. We even managed to hold a few jumble sales in the chapel by putting trestle-table tops on the box pews and serving from behind them. It was not easy, but we needed the money!

These days, with an open-plan building and vastly improved kitchen and toilet facilities, we can hold whatever function we like, as long as we can find a free evening when the chapel is not booked by a group from the town. Don't forget the time-honoured coffee morning: it tends to be under-valued these days, but an informal gathering over a cup of coffee can work wonders for morale. With a modest charge and a raffle or a bring-and-buy stall, it can raise a few pounds for the funds, and everyone has a good time! And there is the annual 'World's Biggest Coffee Morning' in September, organised by the Macmillan Nurses charity. They will send you a pack of instructions, balloons, posters, etc. on request. This way you can get some much-needed extra publicity in the local press and radio with only a little effort.

Why should pubs have all the fun?

I serve the Banbury congregation as their Lay Leader. Meeting for worship only once a month in the Town Hall, they are obliged to rely on house-group meetings for social events, and these work very well indeed. We hold 'Desert Island Discs' evenings, poetry and music evenings, and once a year a mid-day 'Round the World Lunch' in a member's garden, to which people are invited to bring a plate of 'ethnic' food to share. We use these occasions to plan programmes of social events, as well as developing our knowledge of each other and deepening friendships. Once a year we also have a tea-party in a member's garden.

At Warwick we hold many similar activities, plus Fish & Chip Suppers (with the assistance of the local 'chippy') and an annual barbeque in the chapel garden (which we craftily time to coincide with the Castle's open-air fireworks concert, given by the City of Birmingham Symphony Orchestra in the grounds of the nearby castle). We also hold 'Table-Games Evenings', featuring old-fashioned pastimes like snakes and ladders, ludo, card games, and beetle-drives, all of which take very little effort to organise and are most enjoyable. And there are the inevitable quiz evenings, which are so popular in pubs these days – but why should pubs have all the fun?

'Pot-Luck' lunches or suppers take very little organising and yet can be very pleasurable and give folk a feeling of doing things together, which is what it is all about.

Some more ideas for social events

Keep an ear open for members' comments: many a good idea can arise from a throw-away remark. A good few years ago, on a coach-trip to Shugborough Hall, someone in the Warwick congregation mused 'Wouldn't it be nice to go on a country walk some time?' And so our regular rambling group was established, originally meeting on Sunday mornings (because at that time we held only evening services). We took turns to lead a fairly short local walk, about four miles maximum. This group is still going today, about 20 years later, although we have adapted to circumstances in that we now walk only on alternate Sunday mornings, because we hold morning services on the other two Sundays.

We used to hire a coach for chapel outings, to visit places such as stately homes and gardens. But over the years this has become a rather costly enterprise, unless one can be reasonably certain of filling a large coach, so these days we look out for coach companies running commercial trips to places of our liking, and we take a block booking of say, a dozen or so seats – and let someone else have all the work of organising it.

The wife of one of our members remarked to me one day, 'The local Methodists are running *pétanque* sessions, and they are quite popular. We have a good garden, why don't we try it?' English weather being what it is, we decided first of all to try our hands at carpet bowls, which we play diagonally across the chapel (where the felt carpet tiles are ideal for the game). We make up our own rules, and we charge £1 for a two-hour session, with coffee included. When the weather is fine, we play our own version of *boules* or *pétanque* on the chapel lawn, and much hilarity ensues. These days we play fortnightly on a Tuesday afternoon from 2pm to 4pm. Sets of carpet bowls are fairly cheap to buy: around £14 per set of eight. Proper *boules* are rather heavy and more costly, but there are also several plastic sets for purchase, aimed at the seaside market.

Another indoor social event that we occasionally hold in either January or February is an 'OFMIJ' night (**O F**lip **Me It's** January) – or 'OFMIF' if in February. This is an evening of silly games or other items designed to dispel the gloom of winter, maybe coupled with a fancy-dress evening and some humorous poetry or prose, and perhaps a few old-fashioned party games such as 'Pass the Parcel'.

If you have enough members who are not too elderly, you could try a Country Dance evening: borrow some country-dance records from the local library and have a go! Play readings can be interesting, and your local library may be able to supply multiple copies of scripts. We find that anything to do with food is popular: simple fare like baked potatoes and a filling, or sausage and mash. Various members can usually be persuaded to contribute a dish, so that all the work does not fall upon one person. Involving as many as possible will make people feel wanted and useful.

Some churches and chapels, I know, have strong social programmes, but many others do not, and they are missing out on much that can enhance the life of the congregation. I am firmly convinced that socialising is just as valuable as worshipping together, for both are important parts of life, which should not be kept in separate compartments. If the essence of Unitarianism is our interactions one with another, then coffee and chat after the service are as essential as the act of worship itself, in that they give members a chance to develop their relationships and exchange ideas and opinions – which is what we are all about, are we not?

The author

Malcolm Sadler was born into Unitarianism in 1935. At Waverley Road Unitarian Church in Birmingham, he was organist and secretary of the large youth club until 1959, when he took over as organist at Warwick. Over the years he has held many positions, both locally and nationally, currently being secretary of UALL (Unitarian Association of Lay Leaders), secretary / treasurer of Warwickshire and Neighbouring

Counties Monthly Meeting of Protestant Dissenting Ministers (1782), chair of Trustees of Oat Street Chapel, Evesham, and editor of 'MU NOW', the magazine of the Midland Union of Unitarian and Free Christian Churches, besides serving as music director at Warwick Chapel and Lay Leader, Musical Director, and Treasurer of Banbury Unitarian Fellowship.

Questions for reflection and discussion

1. Do you agree that social interaction is a primary purpose of the church community?

2. How highly would you rate the social life of your congregation?

3. Do you agree that the essence of Unitarianism is relationships?

4. Which kinds of social activity work best in a church hall, and which in a private home?

Part Two
Being together in the wider community

9 Congregational life in the city

John Midgley

There is something different about the life of a Unitarian congregation located in a city – by which I mean a city *centre*. Having previously served as a minister in a small town and then in the suburbs (though never in a village), I feel this difference now that I am in a city-centre post, but I find it far from easy to clarify just what it is. One element of the difference is that there is often an underlying tension between the old and the new. The General Assembly Directory shows that most of our city-centre congregations have a seventeenth-century foundation, giving them a long-established, historically rooted feel. Alongside that, just outside their doors, the modern, busy city rushes by, with its latest trends, fashions, and often short-lived current concerns. This sense of our glorious history, often reflecting the days when many of the great and the good, the movers and shakers of civic life, were Unitarians, has been described by one minister as a 'sweet burden'.

As the minister of the oldest non-conformist place of worship in Manchester, I find that the temptation to live off past glories is sweet indeed. However, while being a sort of museum of civic history may be an attractive feature, it is never more than a tiny part of what we are really about. Manchester Unitarians revel in their past, having produced the first ever Mayor of the city, as well as the *Guardian* newspaper and much, much more. We particularly delight in memorials to nineteenth-century novelist Elizabeth Gaskell, wife of Revd William Gaskell, a minister of renown. With glee we show these off when researchers call in, seeking information about local history, or literature, or family trees, or when radio and television companies come to visit. Then we invite them to look at who and what we are *today*, and what we aspire to *become*. That is much harder.

The changing city scene

City centres vary and change. A crucial matter is whether or not they are residential. Some have handsome mansions and streets of houses, tenements, and flats, constituting a potential congregation in the locality. The situation in Manchester, like many others, is in a state of change. In the first half of the twentieth century, people fled the smoky, industrial city for the leafy suburbs, so that by the time of the 1991 census, city-centre Manchester (which is fairly clearly definable) had barely more than four hundred residents. Then, in 1996, a massive terrorist bomb was detonated. There was extensive damage, many injuries, but amazingly no deaths. Little did the perpetrators know that their work would galvanise the resolve of the city planners to move ahead with a major redevelopment. We now have new streets, squares, and shops – and crucially, a re-population programme. The city centre now records nearly fourteen thousand residents, with more to come. Most of them live in flats for single persons or couples, so we are waiting to see if these newcomers will settle into some sort of community life, in which our congregation can play a part. Cross Street Unitarian Chapel has already attracted a few of these new city dwellers. Meanwhile, most of our loyal attenders, for their own reasons, continue to travel in from the suburbs, sometimes from as far as twenty or thirty miles away.

City centres have districts, with their own characteristics. Our city-centre location is in the commercial area, surrounded by banks, building societies, insurance offices, and lawyers' chambers, with the Town Hall, the international concert hall, theatres, convention centres, and fine civic buildings all around. So I look with enormous admiration at courageous Methodist colleagues in another area, just across the city. Theirs is a colourful, cosmopolitan quarter, among the betting shops, pawn-brokers, late-night pubs, and gambling casinos, an Oxfam supermarket, second-hand record shops, old warehouses turned into shopping arcades, and an emporium where you can have your body pierced, massaged, or tattooed. The Methodists have a drop-in, befriending centre for the homeless and rootless, with a food pantry in their cellar. The soup kitchens appear on Saturday nights. We Unitarians are unable to contemplate work like that in our modern, comfortable, state-of-the art building, with its fitted carpets, fully fitted kitchen, and 'all mod cons'. Instead we tap into local cultural activities, by hosting lunchtime classical music recitals. We have attracted high-quality performers from the Hallé Orchestra, the BBC Philharmonic Orchestra, and some university music teachers, students and others. We have had poetry recitals, art exhibitions, and lectures by members of the local Antiquarian Society and the Gaskell Society. We accommodated some major public meetings for the Jubilee 2000 Campaign. Then, at Harvest Festival, we send the Methodists our good wishes and our donations for the food pantry. The Methodists, in turn, envy us our luxurious building.

From the Cathedral to Coronation Street

As well as culture and the arts, city-centre churches can participate in civic life. I receive invitations to the annual Civic Service at the Cathedral and events in the Town Hall, where I have rubbed shoulders with the Lord Mayor, the High Sheriff, the Leader of the Council, the Chief Executive, the Town Clerk, and even, occasionally, visiting members of the Royal Family.

I usually 'robe up' and process with the other ministers and clergy on such occasions. Increasingly I also find myself with representatives of 'other faith communities', as city authorities and the more forward-looking Anglicans at the Cathedral develop multi-faith policies and programmes.

Some of our city churches are sufficiently long established for their ministers to become known figures in the city. For any minister with an appetite for becoming a headline-grabbing 'player' in the city scene, opportunities are there all right, but they require much time and energy (more than I am prepared to give). This can all be made to sound much more impressive than it actually is, but I feel that when opportunities occur, it is good for Unitarians to be up there with the rest. At the same time, it is also good to be known by the local newsvendor, the barrow boys, and the manager of the local sandwich bar. Sometimes it feels just a little like a larger version of *Coronation Street*.

A place for the church in civic forums and the voluntary sector

Like other cities, Manchester has an effective and influential City Centre Management Company, who will contact the churches to discuss matters that may well have a social-justice dimension. This organisation, a sort of quango, is responsible for such things as street markets and the Christmas lights, the flower arrangements on street lamps, and street demonstrations and displays. They also have influence on such matters as local licensing laws. Contacts with such bodies can be valuable, because issues such as 'binge drinking', soup runs in the city, and street parades and sports events that may clash with Sunday church-going all require careful consultation. The minister or a representative member of the congregation may well have an opportunity to put a case. This is often done in conjunction with members of other denominations, as an ecumenical exercise. Unitarians are not always welcome in such forums, but city-centre churches tend to be at the more liberal and inclusive end of the religious spectrum, while the more exclusive, conservative evangelicals are more likely to be found in the suburbs. For the most part, faiths other than Christian are not to be found in great numbers in city centres. They tend to congregate in the suburbs. City-centre Manchester has just one Reform Synagogue, a Buddhist centre, and a tiny upper room for a Mosque.

The 'city feel' inevitably affects the life of a congregation. There is a certain dynamic, a buzz in the air, an almost audible hum. Unitarian congregations can participate in this by being a confident, welcoming, and forward-looking presence, offering worship that is relevant, contemporary, and topical. They can also participate and contribute to community life by providing accommodation for the kinds of activity already described, as well as offering hospitality in the form of lettings to community groups, clubs, and societies. The voluntary sector of city life has a great need of rooms for meetings, conferences, training days, and the like. If nothing else, a Unitarian congregation can gain a reputation, in the world of social-justice concerns, for its willingness to provide such accommodation. We in Manchester have hosted special services for victims of road accidents, for renal-dialysis patients, bereaved parents of infants following still-births or cot deaths, and the regional Townswomen's Guild.

A shop-window for Unitarianism

City churches are often seen as regional centres for the District Associations of the General Assembly of Unitarian and Free Christian Churches. Some are regarded as 'the mother church' of the district, sometimes the 'flag-ship' or 'shop window' for nearby Unitarian congregations. It seems to matter to suburban congregations that the city-centre churches are in good heart and presenting a positive and confident face to the world. Members of city congregations sometimes smile when they contemplate this perspective, knowing that despite (or perhaps because of) their central location, their numbers are often small and their problems great. Buildings need to be managed, with continuous problems related to security, cleaning, and maintenance. Travel and parking difficulties are a constant frustration. Sunday trading has made an impact. For this reason, city churches do not attract many weddings or infant baptisms, or even funeral services. In recent years there has been some growth in requests for same-sex blessing ceremonies. These, too, are perhaps more of an urban phenomenon than a suburban one, but even in Manchester with its 'Gay Village' of some renown, requests for such ceremonies are few and far between.

City churches do attract new members, but these seem often to be on a spiritual journey, glad to stop at this way-station for a while, but then moving on. Turnover of membership tends to be high, making it hard to find those who will take on leadership roles. City-centre congregations tend to be somewhat less cohesive than local religious communities, since members live at great distances and do not often meet mid-week. A steady trickle of tourists, as visitors to Sunday worship, unknown to minister or members, come along and are welcome, although their presence affects the dynamic. City-centre churches often cater for people dropping in, on any and every day, so ministers and others need to spend more time actually on site.

A haven from the hubbub of the city

Much of what has been said here is also true of suburban and small-town congregations, so the difference in the character of city churches remains difficult to pinpoint. We put our main

71

emphasis on worship. In the city, knowing that the nearby Cathedral and the city parish church have salaried music directors and full choirs, our impulse is to offer worship that is distinctly different, but of no less quality.

City chapels and churches can be challenging and exciting places, with much to offer. They require much commitment, patient hard work, and considerable resources. Publicity – whether in the form of posters, literature, or (increasingly) websites – needs to be effective and of high quality. Unitarianism certainly has a place in urban life, offering an alternative to the styles and ideas of more conventional church worship.

Last, but by no means least, a city-centre church can provide what we in Manchester call 'a spiritual oasis in the heart of the city'. Our chapel is becoming known as a haven of peace and quiet amid the hubbub. It can be argued that its serene presence has a symbolic power, as well as a practical one, which is just as important and valuable – perhaps even more so. Congregations such as ours can offer a spiritual alternative to, or haven from, the commercial rat race, by focusing on the preciousness of people in a sometimes harsh, dehumanising world.

The author

Revd John Midgley was born in Birmingham and found his way into Unitarianism as a teenager. He entered the Unitarian ministry in 1966 and is currently minister at Cross Street Chapel, Manchester, having previously served as General Assembly Development Officer and, before that, as minister in Altrincham, Urmston, and Padiham. For twenty years he was a part-time tutor at Unitarian College, Manchester. He was President of the General Assembly from 2001 to 2002. He has qualifications in theology and adult education and community development. His wife Celia is also a Unitarian minister.

Questions for reflection and discussion

1. What is distinctive about a city-centre Unitarian congregation, as compared with congregations located elsewhere?

2. Do Unitarians have a place among the established churches in the cities, working alongside senior churchmen and women, as well as civic authorities and policy makers?

3. What contribution can Unitarian congregations make to the cultural or artistic life of a city?

4. Do Unitarian ministers, or lay-folk in leadership positions, need any special qualities or qualifications in order to feel comfortable in a city-centre location?

10 Healing as well as helping: a step beyond social responsibility

Jo Lane

At the suggestion of the Editor, this chapter was to have been entitled 'Social responsibility and congregations with a purpose'. But I don't like the term *social responsibility*: it sounds wooden and plodding, and it implies a one-way flow of action and benefit. I would prefer to envision and practise a simultaneous, spiralling process of 'outreach' and 'inreach': reaching in to the core of ourselves, touching the compassion that resides there, and reaching out again to the world around us; taking in with open arms all that the world has to offer, and taking that back again to the centre of ourselves. It is a process of paradox and contradiction in which we come to know the truth of both these phrases: *'You cannot love another until you love yourself'*, and *'You find yourself by losing yourself'*.

In deciding which form of outreach/inreach would be most appropriate to our religious community at the Richmond and Putney Unitarian Church, I took the ideas of Mike Riddell and Ram Dass and Mirabai Bush to the congregation. The post-modern Christian theologian Mike Riddell believes that the future of churches lies in small groups that allow for genuine human interaction. He identifies elements that he believes are common to experimental religious ventures that are 'new and hopeful models of being the church' (1998, pp. 157-71). Riddell says that the following qualities are indicators of such models:

1. All place a high premium on relationship. They allow time and space for relating, and do not permit programme time or structure to squeeze it out.

2. There is minimal structure in experimental ventures. High degrees of organisation are regarded as stifling creativity.

3. Human emotion is welcomed and celebrated, with a very loose sense of propriety.

4. The ventures are relatively small; they are wary of growing to a size where the relationships that they value so much may be inhibited. Some of the functions of these communities would not be possible in larger groups.

5. There is an appreciation of and encouragement towards genuine spirituality, recognising that traditional patterns may not always be appropriate in the post-modern world. There is a willingness to draw from whatever sources may be helpful.

6. Such communities provide space and refuge for those who may be battered by the experiences of life. Demands are not placed on participants that they are not ready to meet. Grace is extended so that people may find their own way forward.

Dass and Bush (1992, p. 174) suggest a simple beginning for such ventures: *'start small, start where you are, use what you have got, do something you enjoy and don't over-commit'*.

With these things in mind, we formed a group that we called 'Helping and Healing With Crafts and Stories'. We meet monthly for two hours in the church. The group consists of members of our Richmond congregation, members of three other Unitarian congregations in the London district, and people from the wider community. We span the ages; and we are both men and women. We light a chalice, we have opening words, and each month we take turns, two at a time, to tell a story. Sometimes it is our own story; sometimes it is drawn from elsewhere; and each month as group leader I read something on the social and political history of handwork around the world. We then take ten minutes to knit and sew in meditative silence. We knit for six charities, including a premature-baby unit, nursing homes, and orphanages in the Ukraine; a hospice in West London; a charity providing blankets and clothes for babies who are stillborn; and an organisation providing quilts to children recovering from abusive situations.

The gratitude expressed by those receiving our gifts has been humbling, and the benefits to ourselves, both as individuals and as a religious community, have been deep indeed. Crafting and telling stories together has allowed the soulful qualities of deep listening and nourishing conversation to emerge. It is inspiring to see someone 'find their hands' and 'find their voice', perhaps for the first time. Many talented writers and storytellers among us have found the courage for the first time to share their gifts. Many who have felt themselves unable even to thread a needle have come to know the deep satisfaction of using simple tools and taking pleasure in using texture and colour to make something with their own hands that will bring comfort and pleasure to others. Knitting, sewing, crocheting, and story telling are nurturing crafts, and they are honest ones. The success of our group has been a joy to us all. We are currently exploring the possibility of incorporating another dimension into our group: that of sponsoring a community of women who knit for profit in the developing world, helping them to receive a fair price for their goods.

Our group has started small, begun from where we are, used what we have (in skills and gifts that are considerable), and done something that we have all enjoyed. It has been a wonderful example of the spiralling paradox of inreach and outreach that reaches and touches us all.

References and further reading

Dass, R. and M. Bush (1992) *Compassion In Action: Social and Spiritual Growth and Healing On the Path of Service*, London: Rider

Gyatso, Tenzin (the Fourteenth Dalai Lama) (1984) *Kindness, Clarity and Insight*, New York: Snow Lion

Hartley, M. and J. Ingilby (2001) *The Old Handknitters of the Dales*, Skipton: Dalesman Publishing

Manning, T. (2004) *Mindful Knitting: Inviting Contemplative Practice To The Craft*, Boston: Tuttle

Pinkola-Estes, C. (1994) *The Gift of Story: A Wise Tale About What is Enough*, New York: Ballantine

Riddell, M. (1998) *Threshold of the Future: Reforming the Post-Christian West*, London: SPCK

Schumacher, E.F. (1973) *Small is Beautiful: Economics as if People Mattered*, London: Harper and Row

Sweeney, J. (et al.) (2000) *Praying With Our Hands: Twenty-One Practices of Embodied Prayer From The World's Spiritual Traditions*, Woodstock: Skylight Paths

The author

Revd Jo Lane has been the minister of the Richmond and Putney Unitarian Church since 2000. She grew up in rural South Australia and worked for 15 years as a Registered Nurse. After completing a degree in Comparative Religion at the University of South Australia, Jo moved to the United Kingdom to train for the ministry at Unitarian College Manchester and University College Chester. She is married to Rory, a teacher, and they have two small daughters. Jo's special interests in ministry are pastoral care and working with small groups. Her hobbies are reading and knitting.

Questions for reflection and discussion

1. How do you react to the advice of Dass and Bush on starting a new church venture?

2. What do you think are the factors that have operated in this local church to enable social-responsibility activities to flourish?

3. What do you think is the best way to set up a social-responsibility group in a church?

4. How might we judge the worth of social-responsibility activities undertaken by congregations?

11 One World Centres

Wynne Simister

There are One World Centres in many countries around the world. In the UK, in cities that include Belfast, Dundee, and Hull, the centres support community action for peace and justice by providing resources, premises, and publicity for local, national, and international campaigns and projects.

The One World Centre in Oldham was the idea of Clarice Nuttall, the Chair of Oldham Unitarian Chapel in the early 1990s. Clarice wanted to establish a lasting, living memorial to her late husband Eric, who had died in 1992. In particular she wanted to create something from which disadvantaged people might benefit. When she read in *The Inquirer* about the One World Centre in Lewes, Sussex, this seemed to be just what she was looking for. She and her friend Marian Nuttall visited Jeremy Goring, at that time the Unitarian Minister at Lewes, and were invited to observe a meeting of the committee of the One World Centre there. They received helpful advice from the Lewes committee, and Clarice decided to adopt their aims and objectives as part of her proposal to establish a similar centre in Oldham.

At a meeting held at Oldham Chapel in September 1992, Clarice read out a paper in which she argued that issues of peace, development, social justice, and environmental sustainability 'have some impact on the community, but still remain marginal to the forces of reaction which seem to dominate society as a whole'. Clarice was concerned about the weariness and frustration experienced by the small progressive groups that were active in the area and duplicating each other's efforts. She had a vision of a centre that would provide a focus to channel energies more effectively and demonstrate Unitarians' ability to work with people of other religions and cultures. It could demonstrate a living, outward-looking chapel, genuinely seeking to co-operate with like-minded people. She argued that a One World Centre would increase public awareness of progressive issues, and create a greater sense of identity for the component groups. The groups would retain their own aims and goals, but would benefit from the publicity given to the One World Centre. The chapel committee agreed with Clarice, and our Centre was established ready to celebrate One World Week in October 1992. The sum of £500, given in memory of Eric Nuttall, was used to buy Traidcraft produce and to build a unit to store the goods.

Clarice herself has since died, but the Centre lives on, embodying in the everyday affairs of its supporters her belief that 'the earth is not a possession but a trust'.

What we do in Oldham

The Centre is a non-profit venture. We sell fairly traded goods and organise lunches every Thursday. The food is donated, and the proceeds are given to Third World causes. Over the years many groups have used our premises for meetings. Currently the user groups are mainly concerned with human rights, so for example we host meetings of an organisation called Oldham Unity To Defend Asylum Seekers. A section of this group is devoted to working politically and peacefully against the British National Party (BNP), which is still a force to be reckoned with in Oldham. We host a project for destitute failed asylum seekers, providing the bare essentials of food, clothing, and money to enable them to survive. We also hold a monthly social event for asylum seekers, where they can meet each other and get advice from various support agencies.

We are now a recognised centre for the collection of unwanted tools for the 'Tools for Self-Reliance' scheme, which was set up to meet the needs of poor people to carve out a living in a world where the odds are stacked against them. The tools are refurbished and provided cost-free to village workshops in some of the poorest countries of the world.

Also meeting at the Centre are a women's interfaith group, and another group of women who work to combat racism. A group of Asian women meet regularly on our premises. They campaign against a law which means, as I understand it, that men who bring their wives here from another country effectively have two years in which to reject them. If the wife is rejected during this 'probation period', she can be deported back to her country of origin with her children. In many cases, however, the family of a rejected wife from South Asia will not want her back, because she is deemed to be in disgrace. Meanwhile, she is denied asylum in this country, so she is trapped.

Three religious groups with no meeting place of their own use our chapel: the Dechen Buddhists, the Samatha Buddhists, and the Religious Society of Friends. Our premises are also used by the local branch of Friends Of The Earth, and by the Co-op's member-relations group, which gives grants to community organisations and ethical /social projects. Other users include the Oldham branch of the Manchester and Lancashire Family History Society; 'After Adoption', a support group for people who have recently adopted a child; and 'Floral Art'.

Since Clarice's death in 1999, we have tried to keep her dream alive and to develop it. Marian Nuttall, who took over the task of organising the One World Centre, has a small group of volunteers around her who help with the lunches and decide what to do with the money that is raised. We have begun to include Earth Spirit activities under the One World banner: we have held two Mind/Body/Spirit events, and very successful evenings of reflexology, aromatherapy, and Reiki healing. We are seeking to extend this type of activity. We hope too that in the future we will be able to become more actively engaged in local issues as well as world-wide campaigns. Oldham is a cosmopolitan town with a range of social problems, and as such many of its people are in great need of the support of various agencies, both voluntary and non-voluntary.

Some do's and don'ts

It is not easy to offer advice to anyone interested in setting up a similar venture. What to do and what not to do are very individual matters: a lot depends on your particular situation and your own aspirations. But don't expect that by engaging in such a project the numbers attending your services will increase. As far as I am aware, only one person has joined Oldham Chapel through the One World Centre.

If asked to give advice to other Unitarians who might wish to create a One World Centre, I would encourage them to think that besides being used to promote Unitarianism to the wider population, such a project can become a focus for many worthwhile activities, addressing not only Third World issues, but causes such as animal welfare and environment conservation, as well as more purely local issues and concerns. It can be a practical demonstration of the acceptance of diversity in all its many forms, in peacefully confronting matters of concern in the community, and seeking to resolve them where possible. We have had to deal with hostility from politically opposite factions and work peacefully to reach an understanding with them, based on acceptance of another's right to hold different views. In this I am thinking particularly of the BNP, our commitment to interfaith tolerance, and our belief in everyone's right to be.

Two things above all: first, if you choose to start a One World Centre you must be prepared to work hard on many levels, promoting its aims and objectives in the local community, encouraging other groups to join you, and taking part in local campaigns. And second, for the project to be sustainable the whole congregation must be in agreement with its aims and objectives, and willing to work together as a team in order to realise them.

The author

Wynne Simister is the President of the Unitarian congregation in Oldham, and also the organist there. She discovered Unitarianism during her student days but did not become involved in the activities of the denomination until later in life, when she rediscovered it though her work for animal welfare.

Questions for reflection and discussion

1. What are some of the factors that should determine how Unitarian premises are used?

2. Should belief in 'One World' be central to Unitarian thinking and practice?

3. Is supporting Fair Trade a lifestyle choice, or a moral necessity?

4. What steps can a congregation take to develop a distinct role for itself within the local community?

12 The congregation as a community focus

Celia M. Cartwright

One of my favourite books is *The Prophet*, by Kahlil Gibran. The eponymous hero of this story has been waiting for 12 years in the city of Orphalese for the ship that brought him there to return to take him home. One morning the prophet sees the sails of his ship and he knows that his waiting is over. The people of Orphalese, fearing to lose their wise prophet, flock to his side to seek his guidance, asking his advice on every major and minor aspect of their lives. As the dusk begins to fall, someone asks the prophet to speak about religion. In a voice which seems to express irritation and sadness – and perhaps a weary recognition of the fact that some folk just don't get it – the prophet explains that everything that he has talked about is religion. He explains that life cannot be divided into different categories labelled 'soul' and 'body', but that everything we do and say and think is a part of our religion – and when we deny this, we disgrace our faith.

The sacred and the secular

In my view, any congregation that believes that it needs only to tend its soul in the quiet of the sanctuary is a congregation that will not make sense of the world – for it has turned its back on the world. The members of such a congregation, despite all their Sunday worship, just don't get it! They don't get the fact that even though they may be in a minority who attend church, that church is not separate from, but part of, the wider community – part of the world – and to seek to exist outside it is to deny the reality of religion. As we enter the twenty-first century and our society becomes ever more secular, creating a focus for the wider community may be more difficult than it was 50 or 100 years ago; but it is still very necessary, and I believe that most of our Unitarian congregations do actively seek to draw the wider community to their doors, in ways that are many and various.

I would not suggest that Unitarian congregations seek to create a focus for the wider community purely out of a sense of altruism or piety. It must be acknowledged that we are motivated also by the need to raise funds to maintain the very fabric of our buildings, and to pay for the ministry that we desire. But to become a focus for the wider community entails more than raffle tickets and room lettings, and more than a debit and credit balance. Our outreach to the local community, if it is to be successful, must be based on our shared interests: the needs of the wider community must be met in tandem with the needs of the congregation. There must be a willingness to share with and learn from those who are not part of the worshipping community, and we must each be open to the other's needs. Each congregation must create the focus for its own particular community in its own particular way: there is no common blueprint for success.

The 'Units' of Rochdale

Until recently I served the congregation in Rochdale, where the Unitarian church and its congregation have enjoyed a high profile in the town and provided a strong focus for the surrounding community for well over a century. In the nineteenth century the church became known as 'the Co-op Chapel', on account of the fact that a large proportion of the original founders of the Co-operative Association were members of our congregation or shared our non-conformist values.

The congregation's central role in the town and their positive relationship with the community still continue: they even have a pet name! A great number of Rochdale's citizens refer to the church and congregation as 'the Units', so comfortable are they with our place of worship and our people. Those who refer to the congregation in this way are not necessarily part of the worshipping community, but rather those outside who associate the church with social functions such as dances, fund-raising lunches, whist and bridge drives, or simply a meeting place for such diverse groups as a Bowls Club, the Ramblers' Association, the window cleaners of the town, the University of the Third Age, the Soroptimists, and others.

Rochdale is a good example of the way in which a strong congregation, with a purpose-built church, can provide a clear focus for the wider community. Rochdale's practices and attributes, however, are neither universal nor definitive. Each individual congregation relates to its surrounding community in response to particular local needs, in ways that are determined by the skills and abilities of its own members and the nature of its own facilities. However, at the core of each congregation is religion, and we must live our religion '24/7' (to use the modern idiom), using our loyalty to our own church as a basis from which to reach out beyond our own needs and concerns.

Before a congregation is capable of creating a focus for those in the community who do not choose to attend its services, it must learn how to become a clear focus for its own members. That focus begins with the first gathering of a group of people drawn by the prospect of shared beliefs and philosophies, who need each other for spiritual, emotional, practical, and social support. Few of us are 'born Unitarians': we become Unitarian by deliberation, thought, reasoning, questing, testing, practice, sharing beliefs, researching, and learning. Being a Unitarian is a conscious decision: there is no set dogma to follow. We must each use our own powers of reason, and our faith must be fluid and open to change as new insights are gained. Being part of a congregation in which there is a sharing of faith, beliefs, and philosophies will influence the way in which the members respond and react to others, both within and outside the congregation.

Rites of passage ...

In the beginning, such a community meets primarily to worship, an act which may in itself create a focus for the wider community, helping people to share joys and sorrows in the rites of passage that accompany them through life: the bringing of children for baptism or welcome, the joining of two people in marriage, the final celebration at the end of a life, and a space to share mourning and memory. As an extension of this relatively narrow (though most important) private focus, the congregation may also serve the wider community at times of more universal celebrations and commemorations, when a whole society answers the urge to gather together in response to major world events; to respond to the terrible natural and man-made disasters that beset us, such as the tsunami that struck the Indian Ocean region in December 2004, or the day that has become known simply as '9/11', when a terrorist act brought down the twin towers of the World Trade Center in New York; or to share the shock and grief of a tragedy such as the Dunblane massacre, when a gunman ran amok in a school. At such times the presence of an established worshipping community may serve as a focus for a wider community that is unused to seeking spiritual support.

... raffle tickets and room lettings ...

I suggested above that being a focus for the wider community requires more than raffle tickets and room lettings, but there is in every church or chapel congregation a common and major concern, which is the necessity to raise funds to keep the fabric of the building intact and to maintain some form of ministry for its people. 'Live giving', that is to say the money that people contribute to the Sunday collection, contribute as membership subscriptions, and offer as donations, is not, in the main, enough. Many people place in the offertory plate less than the price of a cup of coffee in a café. In Britain, we have not embraced the notion of tithing to raise funds, as have many of our North American churches, nor are most of us blessed with a wealthy philanthropist in our midst to supplement our funds. What we do have is a tradition of volunteering to work together to raise the money that we need to maintain our existence as we want it. But, although the focus may be seen as one of simply raising money, fund-raising can serve as a strong bridge to the wider community and as a bond within the worshipping community. Working together for the benefit of all cements relationships, builds friendships, and creates a sense of purpose and strength and fun – whether in the planning stage, gathering together to pool ideas and skills, or in the implementation stage, with everybody playing their own part, working with those around them to make the event or function a success.

... and religion in action

So far I have addressed the way in which a congregation can become a focus for the community that it creates within the church, and for the wider community that uses its practical and spiritual facilities. But there is another and different way in which the congregation may become a community focus: when the congregation seeks simply, as a charitable act, to serve some part of its community, to fill a gap, to help, or to give. To give time, energy, and financial support becomes a focus for the worshipping community, and for many congregations this serves to make sense of its very existence. Following a service that I conducted about the need to nurture our souls in quiet and reflective ways, I was challenged by a member of my congregation at Rochdale who told me that for him the spirit is nurtured through action. He went on to say that if his congregation were not involved in charitable work, he would find no reason to come to church at all.

For almost 30 years a group of Rochdale's congregation have raised funds and given practical support to the first 'Stroke Group' in the town. In the beginning they answered a dire need for a space where isolated people disabled by strokes might gather together with their carers for mutual support and companionship. Today, the congregation continues to support and share in the life of this group. It is part of the church's annual work to raise funds for charitable causes. The Junior Church President chooses a charity, and the young people set about raising funds; the Women's League members support their own annual charity; the congregation as a whole chooses several charities to support during the year and will make extra efforts when necessary to raise money for global disaster funds. Members of the congregation collect toys and deliver them to a local children's respite-care home; they also collect and deliver food, clothing, and bedding for a Manchester charity for homeless people. Such work represents a focus on the needs of a community beyond the sanctuary, and the Rochdale congregation believes that such acts have their own spiritual function.

If a church congregation does not serve as a focus for the wider community, it fails in its primary role and becomes a closed social club. We are part of the world, we who attend church, who consider ourselves part of a congregation, and we have a responsibility to take the insights that we gain in communion with each other and make of them a focus that will draw others in. Religion should pervade every aspect of our lives, not as a dogmatic structure created to change the world, but rather as an open forum in which we embrace the world, so that we and the world might fear each other less and thus live together in harmony.

Sources and references

Buehrens, John A. and Forrest Church (1998) *A Chosen Faith* (part 4, 'Neighbourhood'), Boston, MA: Beacon Press

Gibran, Kahlil (1923) *The Prophet* (section 24, 'Religion'), New York: Knopf

Keen, Sam (1997) *Hymns to an Unknown God* (part 10, 'The Public Spirit'), London: Piatkus Books

Smith, Matthew (ed.) (2002) *Prospects for the Unitarian Movement* (chapters 8, 12, 14), London: The Lindsey Press

The author

Born in Lancashire, Revd Celia Cartwright has lived in nine counties and two countries. She attended Manchester University and Unitarian College Manchester in her forties, receiving a BA (Hons) and a college certificate in 1997. In 1998 she accepted the invitation of the Rochdale Unitarian congregation to serve as their Minister. She gained a Diploma in Counselling in 2003. She currently serves as President of the Provincial Assembly, and also as the President of the Unitarian Association of Lay Leaders. Since June 2006 she has served as Minister to the Unitarian community in Kendal.

Questions for reflection and discussion

1. In what ways can your own congregation be said to provide a focus for the community?

2. Does your church have a role to play in providing rites-of-passage ceremonies, and /or as a place of spiritual solace in times of national tragedy?

3. Do you agree that fund raising can serve to unite the community?

4. Is it better for a congregation to support one charity over many years, or different charitable causes each year?

Part Three
New ways of being together

13 The Internet: being together online

Deborah J. Weiner

In his poem entitled 'We Arrive Out of Many Singular Rooms', the late Revd Kenneth Patton wrote:

> We arrive out of many singular rooms, walking over the branching streets.
> We come to be assured that brothers and sister surround us, to restore their images on our eyes.
> We enlarge our voices in common speaking and singing.
> We try again that solitude found in the midst of those who with us seek their hidden reckonings.
> ... It is good to be with one another.

How will we *be together* in our congregations in the twenty-first century? How can we *be* together when we meet together in virtual space and time, over the Internet?

Only a few years ago, the world was a different place, and ministry occurred, as Patton envisioned it, in rooms where we could feel the warmth of one another's hands, where we could look into each other's eyes. Indeed, the model of ministry with which I was raised as a Unitarian Universalist child was one of face-to-face, one-to-one ministry. But about ten years ago, that model began to change in remarkable and compelling ways.

In 1995 I worked for the Unitarian Universalist Association (UUA) as Director of Public Relations, Marketing, and Information. Back then, although we had computers for our work, few of us had email addresses; we sent out broadcast information by Western Union Mailgram, and the telephone was our primary means of reaching people immediately. But when the Oklahoma City bombings occurred in April of that year, I found out the news through a chilling email that flashed on my computer screen, sent by a UU named Robert Hurst. He, along with probably 1,000 other Unitarians and Universalists around the world, used email for communication. I had recently decided that I had best get on board that fast-moving train. Hurst, in a series of email messages sent to a list called uus-l, wrote:

> *Somebody just blew up Oklahoma City. We're just a medium-sized city in the middle of the country. Not a particularly important place, not a rich place, not even a place divided by racial tensions. This morning somebody planted a bomb in the Federal Building. It shook my house 5 miles away and blew off the entire front of the building. The injured are already in the hundreds. The TV is a scene of mass chaos, bloody people everywhere. I've always been an existentialist and believed that all we had to protect us against the cold, existentialist winds of the universe was the campfire and our fellows around it. Today I feel as if someone in that circle poured water on the fire. I feel lost, as if everything I believed and held true is nonsense, illusion. I'll be OK, but I'll never be the same.*

That message was stunning in its account of what had happened. In 1995 there was no cnn.com to turn to, no newyorktimes.com, no instant way to find out what was going on, except fuzzy radio stations and the TV. But there was this amazing thing: the Internet.

From nearly that moment on, I began to see the potential of the Internet for galvanising and supporting congregational life. Messages poured in from Unitarians and Universalists all over the world, directed to the members of the Oklahoma City congregation: letters of support, prayers, lamentations. They filled the bulletin board of the church, and they were read on the air on NBC-TV's programme 'Dateline with Jane Pauley'. Ministry arrived in each post and was spread like lightning across the dial-up connections that hooked us – individuals and congregations – to this remarkable tool.

Stronger, healthier congregations

In 1996 there were 61 million Internet users worldwide. By April 1997 there were 80 million users, and around that time the first easily accessible version of the UUA's website was created, thanks to the efforts of a group of volunteers who executed a design developed by a staff group who had a vision of an attractive and welcoming site. Our first email list on uua.org was created in February 1995, designed to bring people of one of our districts into closer contact. Today, we have nearly 275 email lists, with more than 20,000 unique addresses subscribing; this number grows day by day. Some lists are used for the sharing of denominational news, information, and resources; others enable topical discussions to take place: for example, leaders of our larger congregations discuss governance, and members of rural congregations talk about techniques for attracting new members. All these lists help to build strength and health in our congregations.

We have been able to develop our ministry and support of one another through other electronic means as well. Starting in 1996, when a volunteer, Jim Mason, built the first version of a UUA website to use html, links and graphics, we began to offer an increasing amount of coverage of our General Assembly, which is our annual denomination meeting. We began with a few digital images and reports, but quickly, as demand grew for our services and our documentation of activities at GA, our efforts expanded. We now have a volunteer staff of nearly twenty, which augments our paid staff at GA, offering twenty-plus hours of live streaming media of our plenaries, major lectures, and worship services, as well as reports of hundreds of workshops and programmes.

One of our most valued elements at General Assembly is coverage and simulcast of our Service of the Living Tradition, and our Sunday worship service. Two years ago, for example, we received messages from Barcelona in Spain and from Ferry Beach in Maine, where people were watching the streaming. In Middlebury, Vermont, UUs gathered in a home, hooking up the computer to the TV so that they could watch the video in large-screen format. In Ferry Beach, one of the ministers who was being welcomed into fellowship but was unable to travel to Long Beach, California, watched the Service of the Living Tradition on screen; when her name was read out, she walked across the room to 'receive her certificate', to the applause of those present. Powerful stuff. Life-changing.

A new way of ministering to one another

The sermons that we archive on our General Assembly site are among the most frequently read material that we offer, and video files of our worship services take the highest number of hits on our site – for good reason: people are hungry for ministry, and this is how we literally serve it up.

Small-group ministry, also known as 'covenant group ministry', has taken hold in a huge way within Unitarian Universalism over the last few years, and this, too, has shaped our ministry through the Internet. We have an email list for covenant-group leaders and those interested in learning more about this important way of establishing close connection and deepening faith in small groups. And a couple of years ago, the UUA published a book by Revd Robert Hill on this subject: *Small Group Ministry: Saving the World Ten at a Time* has been a huge seller. We are all ministers, and we can all contribute to the spiritual development of our brothers and sisters in community.

Researcher Norman Nie of Stanford University said in the findings of his landmark study of Internet culture, published in 2000, 'There are going to be millions of people with very minimal human interaction ... No one is asking ... what kind of world we are going to live in when the Internet becomes ubiquitous.' But, as sociologist Amitai Etzioni observed in the same year about the same culture, 'People do form very strong relations over the internet ... many ... are relations that they could not find in any other way.'

Into this culture, then, came the developing World Wide Web and Unitarian Universalism's continuing exploration of the ways in which religious organisations might use this powerful tool. It was Steve Waldman, founder of beliefnet.com, who observed: 'God is almost as big as sex.' And the *New York Times* published research late in the year 2000 from a study by the Pew Charitable Trust which stated that 21 per cent of Americans went online to find religions or religious information – more than the numbers of people who did online banking. Religion on the Web is non-judgmental, anonymous unless you wish it otherwise, and available 24 hours a day. We find that, on any Sunday, more than 300 distinct Internet addresses visit the UUA's website, where links to the websites of more than 85 per cent of all our congregations can be found. These people are looking for a church to attend, and we can offer them information with direct links to our congregations, almost all of whom have links on our website. What a powerful tool this is! When the attacks of September 11th 2001 occurred, our website was of huge use to thousands of people, including many who were not Unitarian Universalists. In 2003 we were notified that the Minerva project of the Library of Congress had chosen our website for preservation as part of the permanent archive of web resources developed in the aftermath of the events of September 11th. Since that time, through the Iraq War and other major events that have shaped our lives as citizens of the world, the Web has been there, forcing us to re-imagine how we minister to one another.

But ministry it surely is, ministry that can support and enhance what our congregations offer. There are more than one thousand Unitarian Universalist member congregations, and nearly all of them have websites – some good, some bad, some ugly. Those sites are all linked from our website at the UUA; they thus provide a way for individuals who are looking for a church to find out more about what a particular congregation can offer. Similarly those church websites allow the members and friends of a congregation to stay in touch with the congregation's latest news, events, and ministry. It is a remarkable, real-time tool, with the power to reach out and take us by the hand and minister to our needs.

'More power, more understanding, more harmony'

This effort, like so much about the Internet, continues to evolve. We are learning, sometimes through painful experiences and the turning of a world that can seem mad, how to use the tools that we have been given. Sir Tim Berners-Lee, the Unitarian Universalist who created the World Wide Web in 1991, wrote that people of our faith tradition are called to accept 'the useful parts of philosophy from all religions, including Christianity and Judaism...Hinduism, Buddhism, and [other] philosophies, and wrap them...into an environment in which people think and discuss, argue, and always try to be accepting of differences of opinion and ideas'. Those tenets, which also shape life in our congregations, are the ones that have determined the UUA's policies for email lists hosted on our website, and indeed they guide the elements that we try to offer on the web. Berners-Lee said of this remarkably powerful medium that he created,

> Hope in life comes from the interconnections among all the people in the world. We believe that if we all work for what we think individually is good, then we as a whole will achieve more power, more understanding, more harmony as we continue the journey.

These thoughts are the ones that guide us on the journey that we have taken in the UUA Office of Electronic Communication, towards creating a powerful religious community and a way to offer real ministry in real time. I am convinced that the Internet, when used with intentionality and dedication to the mission of our free faith, is one of our most powerful tools for spreading the good word and inviting others in.

Suggestions for further reading

Cann, Tony and George D. Chryssides (2003)'Unitarians and the Internet', in *Unitarian Perspectives on Contemporary Social Issues*, edited by George D. Chryssides, London: The Lindsey Press

Hill, Robert L. (2003) *The Complete Guide to Small Group Ministry: Saving the World Ten At a Time*, Boston, MA: Skinner House Books

Taylor, Kate (2002) 'The Unitarian on-line community', in *Prospects for the Unitarian Movement*, edited by Matthew F. Smith, London: The Lindsey Press, 2002

The author

Deborah Weiner is the Director of Electronic Communication for the Unitarian Universalist Association, based in Boston, Massachusetts. She is a lifelong Unitarian Universalist who has worked with congregations and groups in the USA and internationally on issues of growth, communication, and outreach. Formerly an arts administrator and radio broadcaster, Deborah has been with the UUA for more than fifteen years, working in public relations, marketing, and communications.

Questions for reflection and discussion

1. Does the Internet currently play a part in your involvement with Unitarianism? If so, how?

2. In what ways might the Internet be a useful tool for congregations?

3. Should the Internet be used to create online religious communities, or only to support face-to-face congregations?

4. Does the Internet fit with or run counter to Unitarian values?

14 Dialogue as a form of spiritual practice

Peter Hawkins

Throughout known human history, communities have come together in some form of communal spiritual practice. The form of the practice is determined by where that society locates its God, or its sense of the divine. Animist or pantheist societies would make offerings to the Gods as embodied in the natural world. Those who located God in a transcendent heaven would build temples and worship their deity there. Those who located the divine within the individual human soul developed forms of worship such as prayer, contemplation, meditation, and listening to one's conscience, all of which supported their aspiration to turn inwards and listen to 'the God within'.

A religion centred on relationships

Now there is an increasing interest in locating the divine in the relationships *between* us, in both human-to-human relationships and relationships with and between natural elements and forces. Raimon Panikkar (quoted in Hall 2004) writes:

> God is neither within you nor among you, but between you.
> Everything in the world is interrelated, and beings themselves are nothing but relations.

When we locate the divine in the connections between us, we need to have forms of being together that attend to this aspect of religion.

In other fields also there has been an increasing emphasis on the relational aspects of being. In psychotherapy there is a growing interest in 'intersubjective psychotherapy' (Stolorow *et al.* 1994) and 'dialogical therapy' (Jacobs 1995); in education, Paulo Freire pioneered the centrality of dialogue in the learning process. David Bohm, the nuclear physicist and follower of Krishnamurti, saw dialogue as critical to creating the social transformation that is needed in human beings. And Peter Senge, Bill Issacs, Meg Wheatley, Nancy Dixon, Patricia Shaw, and I myself have developed dialogue in the field of organisational development.

Dialogical approaches have been formulated also in the field of interfaith and religious development. Panikkar (quoted above) writes about the need to move from *dialectical dialogue*, which seeks to convert another to one's own point of view, to *dialogical dialogue*. He describes dialogical dialogue in the following terms:

> Opening myself to another so that he might speak and reveal my myth that I cannot know by myself because it is transparent to me, and appears self-evident. A myth is something in which you believe, without believing that you believe in it. One who aids us in demythicizing our myth actually forces us to establish new myths. People cannot live without myths nor without changing myths, and in dialogical dialogue we are able to experience this truth. (Panikkar 1995, p. ix, quoted in Hall 2004)

All of life can be seen as a learning process, and learning can be seen as relational and requiring dialogue. The wise fool Nasrudin, when asked how he became so wise, replied: 'It is easy, I just talk a lot, and when I see people nodding their heads, I write down what I have said' (Hawkins 2005).

Defining dialogue

David Bohm (1996) defined dialogue as follows:

> The word dialogue is based on the Greek 'dia', meaning 'through', and 'logos', meaning 'the word'. But what is signified here is not the word as such (i.e. the sound), but its meaning. **Dialogue is a free flow of meaning between people.** We may use here the image of a stream flowing between two banks.

> What is essential for dialogue is that while a person may prefer a certain position, a person does not hold to it non-negotiably. Such a person is ready to listen to others with sufficient sympathy and interest to understand the meaning of the other's position properly, and is ready to change his or her own point of view if there is good reason to do so. Evidently a spirit of goodwill or friendship is necessary for this to take place. It is not compatible with a spirit that is competitive, contentious, or aggressive.

> [Dialogue] will happen when people are able to face their disagreements without either confrontation or polite avoidance of the issue, and when they are willing to explore together points of view to which they may not personally subscribe.

Bill Issacs (1999) defines dialogue as 'a conversation with a center, not sides'. He continues:

> It is a way of taking the energy of our differences and channelling it toward something that has never been created before. It lifts us out of polarization and into a greater common sense, and is thereby a means for accessing the intelligence and coordinated power of groups of people.
> (Issacs 1999, p.19)

Paulo Freire, who was a radical educator in South America in the 1960s and 1970s, used dialogue as the basis for creating the most effective literacy programme that has ever been developed. His programme not only achieved literacy for large numbers of marginalised people, but it prompted a massive shift in the way in which the poor viewed themselves and the world around them. In short, it was a process of transforming consciousness that led to the empowerment of powerless people. Freire (1994) claimed that 'To speak a true word is to transform the world'.

Learning to dialogue

The ability to dialogue starts with being able to listen, both to others and to oneself. Listening is something that most of us believe we know how to do, but to do it well takes a lifetime to learn. As a psychotherapist I learned and taught listening skills to others; but when eventually I worked in organisational development and found myself teaching factory managers and senior auditors about listening, I was really challenged to explain different types of listening in a way that they could understand and appreciate. I developed a definition of four levels of listening, based on the experiences of the person who is being listened to. The definition is summarised in Table 1.

I shall never forget the time when I was teaching this to a group of very senior partners in one of the top five global professional services firms, and one partner said to me with enormous feeling: 'I wish someone had taught this to me many years ago, as it could have saved me two costly divorces and a lot of pain.' Asked to say more, he continued: 'Well, my ex-wives used to say I was not listening to them, and I would tell them they were wrong and prove it, by repeating what they had told me. Now I realise they were talking about Level 3 listening, and I was talking about Level 2.'

Listening is just the first step. Secondly, as Freire taught, we each must bring the qualities of humility, love, faith, hope, and

Table 1: Four levels of listening

Level of listening	Activity of listener	Outcome in the person being listened to
1. Attending	Eye contact and posture demonstrate interest in the other.	*'This person wants to listen to me.'*
2. Accurate listening	As above, plus accurately paraphrasing what the other is saying.	*'This person hears and understands what I am talking about.'*
3. Empathic listening	Both the above, plus matching the other's non-verbal cues, sensory frame, and metaphors; feeling into their position	*'This person feels what it is like to be in my position, he/she gets my reality.'*
4. Generative empathic listening	All the above, plus using your own intuition and feelings to play back to the other person a fuller version of what you have heard.	*'This person helps me to hear myself more fully than I can by myself.'*

critical thinking to a dialogical encounter. The third step is to learn to listen to our own responses, rather than react from them. In dialogue we notice what thoughts and feelings stir within us when someone else speaks, and we try to suspend judgement and instead use our own responses in order to understand the other more deeply, and also to learn about our own reactions, prejudices, and beliefs.

For dialogue to become a spiritual practice, there is a fifth level of listening that needs to be engaged, to create what

Blake (1996) has called *trialogue*. Here the participants hold open the possibility of a third position. This position, not occupied by any single individual, can be seen as the place of collective witness; or the opening for grace to enter; or, if one is a Christian, the place where the Christ-energy enters *('Where two or three are gathered together in my name, there I will be also'* – Matthew 18: 20*)*. In trialogue we try not only to imagine the reality of the other within us, but also to create the space for grace. We try to be open to learning and meaning that neither of us could possibly have known before we came into disciplined relationship, one with another. Trialogue can be defined as follows: *A dialogue that not only involves two or more people but also involves listening and attending to the sacred that emerges from beyond the personal and inter-personal domains.*

My favourite definition of the sacred comes from Gregory Bateson, who describes the sacred as *'a sense of the whole, which can only be met with awe ...and which inspires humility'* (Bateson and Bateson 1987, p.148). Therefore to listen to God, we have to listen not only to our own inner voice, not only empathically to others, but also to the spaces between us; to listen for what is trying to emerge in the flow of conversation between us, which is originated by no one, and yet can illumine all parties.

The spiritual practice of dialogue

We can engage in the spiritual practice of dialogue in our everyday conversation at work, at home, or in our fellowships and congregations. In a church committee meeting when there is a stuck dispute, we can pause and in silence attune to a collective viewpoint, a higher spirit which transcends our personal views. Then we can each share images, feelings, or sentiments that came to us in the silence. This can move the discussion to a deeper and less confrontational level.

With our life partner or a friend, we can practise listening more deeply to their experience, and paying attention also to the relationship that exists in so many ways and levels between us. We can ask: 'If this relationship had a voice, what would it say to us both?' Instead of asking what you each want from a relationship, try asking: 'What does the relationship need and want from each of us?' Or 'Where does the sacred have life in our relationship?'

Another simple practice, one that is used in Western Buddhist enlightenment practice, is to ask the same question several times, allowing the other person to hear their own answers and then deepen their next response, rather than staying with their first thought. Couples can take it in turns to ask the questions and to be the one who responds. Useful questions for such a practice include the following:

- What is the purpose of your life?
- What do you most long for?
- What is love?
- What is truth?
- What is worthwhile?
- Where do you most closely experience God?

In a group such as a congregation, one can divide into pairs or threes for such practice. In threes the third person listens to the question and the answers and, if required, records them.

Another approach is for the congregation or other group to gather in a circle and, adopting the practices and attitudes described above, engage in a dialogue on a subject such as the following:

- How can we engage more fully together?
- How can we best serve our wider community?
- What can be done to create greater peace in the world?
- What sort of social action would create a better world?

- How can we deepen our individual and collective spirituality?
- How can we as human beings live in greater harmony with the world around us?

The intent in this collective conversation is to listen for the emergence of new thinking that is beyond the exchange of beliefs previously held by those present, to give space for the greater wisdom of the collective to emerge in the spaces between us.

Finally, we can learn to live more dialogically. Step One is to attempt to start every meeting with another person (or indeed every encounter with our garden or with nature) by being as fully present as possible, and attending to what the other has to communicate to us, both verbally and non-verbally. Step Two is to witness our responses, thoughts, and feelings while attending to the other, and to share these fully with the other. Step Three is to listen to the spaces between us and allow the space for grace.

Note

Some of this chapter previously appeared as articles written by Peter Hawkins and published in *The Inquirer* in the series entitled 'Street Spirituality', 2002–2004.

Sources and suggested reading

Bateson, G. and M. C. Bateson (1987) *Angels Fear: An Investigation into the Nature and the Meaning of the Sacred,* New York: Macmillan

Blake, A. (1996) *The Intelligent Enneagram,* London: Shambhala

Bohm, D. (1994) *Thought as System,* London: Routledge

Bohm, D. (1996) *On Dialogue,* London: Routledge

Dixon, Nancy, M. (1998) *Dialogue at Work: Making Talk Developmental for People and Organizations,* London: Lemos and Crane

Freire, P. (1970) *Pedagogy of the Oppressed*, New York: Seabury Press

Freire, P. (1994) *Pedagogy of the Oppressed* (revised edition), New York: Continuum

Hall, Gerard (2004) 'Multi-faith dialogue in conversation with Raimon Panikkar', *Australian E Journal of Theology*, February 2004, issue 2

Hawkins, P. (2005) *The Wise Fool's Guide to Leadership*, London: O Books

Issacs, W. (1999) *Dialogue and the Art of Thinking Together,* New York: Currency

Jacobs, L. (1995) 'Dialogue in gestalt theory and therapy' in R. Hycner and L. Jacobs (eds.) *The Healing Relationship in Gestalt Therapy*, New York: The Gestalt Journal Press

Panikkar, Raimon (1995) *Invisible Harmony; Essays on Contemplation and Responsibility,* Fortress Press

Senge, P. (1990) *The Fifth Discipline: The Art and Practice of the Learning Organization*, New York: Doubleday/Currency

Shaw, P. (2002) *Changing Conversations in Organizations: A Complexity Approach to Change,* London: Routledge

Stolorow, R.D.G. and E. Attwood *et al.* (1994) *The Intersubjective Perspective*, Northvale, New Jersey: Jason Aronson

Wheatley, M. (2002) *Turning to One Another. Conversations to Restore Hope to the Future,* San Francisco: Berret-Keohler

The author

Dr Peter Hawkins is Chairman of Bath Consultancy Group, (www.bathconsultancygroup.com), through whom he works with organisations throughout the world, helping them to align their strategy, culture, and leadership. He is the author of *The Wise Fool's Guide to Leadership* (O. Books, 2005) and co-author of *Supervision in the Helping Professions* (3rd edition, Open University Press, 2006) and *Coaching, Mentoring and Organizational Consultancy: Supervision and Development* (Open

University Press, 2006). He has also published a number of chapters and articles on Unitarian and Sufi spirituality. He is a member of the Bath Unitarian Fellowship, a Hibbert Trustee, and leader of the Bath Sufi Way Circle.

Questions for reflection and discussion

1. How does true dialogue differ from debate or discussion?

2. In what ways might dialogue be used and developed in the Unitarian context?

3. What is necessary for dialogue to move beyond false consensus?

4. What might be a good starting point for you and your congregation?

15 What can be learned from Fellowships?

Karen Hanley

In mainstream British society there seems to be a general move away from patterns of regular worship in religious buildings. Yet within many people there is a deep need for spiritual connections – a need perceived by the psychologist, Carl Jung, in his book *Modern Man in Search of a Soul*. A recent survey has shown that currently most people between the ages of 25 and 47 are too busy with career, family, and home-making to engage in voluntary or community activities; but from the age of 48 onwards they are more likely to be looking to join societies that could give them something that they have long yearned for. It may be that, within the Unitarian movement, the needs of this spiritually hungry group of 48+ people can be answered by the establishment of Fellowships.

The experience of 'being together' is one core value of Unitarian Fellowships in the UK. But what exactly are they? Webster's Dictionary offers the following definitions of 'fellowship': *community of interest, activity, feeling or experience; a company of equals or friends.* More specifically, in a Unitarian context, the General Assembly's constitution indicates that a Fellowship seeking full GA recognition is a worshipping group with at least 12 members, and probably with no building or minister of its own.

Currently Unitarian Fellowships are meeting in members' homes, Quaker meeting houses, and secular premises. Their activities include making music together, singing, discussing books, and reading poetry; going for walks and trips to the cinema; spirituality exercises, meditation, discussion and dialogue groups; bring-and-share meals; and interfaith, ecumenical, and campaigning events, organised jointly with other groups. At least one Fellowship arranges an annual weekend at the Nightingale Centre, Great Hucklow. Last but by no means least is worship, often with a 'kaleidoscope' service to which all the members of the congregation contribute; or a more traditional service, led by a lay leader or lay preacher or, occasionally, a minister.

There are many paths to worship. Doorways are opened to something beyond us when we hear certain pieces of music or poetry, or share listening moments with a friend or stranger. Worship is much wider than the confines of a formal religious service; in all our Fellowship activities we can choose to pause for silence, meditation, reflection, prayer – and we can take time to speak opening or closing words of dedication or blessing at any kind of meeting.

A safe space

There is a continuum of Unitarian presence in the United Kingdom, ranging from individuals to informal groups, to Fellowships, to congregations. Individuals may move in either direction along this continuum as their circumstances change. Some people prefer a smaller, more informal religious community; for them, involvement with Fellowships is a preferred form of Unitarian witness. In the words of Jane Howarth, of the General Assembly's Fellowships Initiative Group:

> People joining fellowships from outside the denomination are seeking to meet needs, and will only settle and develop as participating members of the fellowship if they are comfortable with the way in which their needs are met. It is not merely a

matter of being comfortable with the Unitarian approach, or theology. Fellowships offer an opportunity to reach people who would not join a church even though they might be in sympathy with everything it stood for.

(FIG, 2000)

Fellowship meetings can offer a safe space for people to go forward on their own spiritual journey, in the company of others, without encountering criticism of their beliefs. Fellowship meetings offer an opportunity to recall, with fondness and appreciation, absent members and perhaps to light candles representing 'joys and concerns', to heighten the awareness of being in relationship with others. Reflecting on his experience of one Fellowship, Timothy Powell observed that 'the offering of a non-worship spiritual space is a more fitting and viable role than ... less well attended monthly worship' (2005).

Fellowships are meeting a wide range of needs and can serve several different constituencies:

- their members – by offering an enriching experience that creates opportunities to grow in awareness;
- people in the local community – by offering space for spiritual development and support;
- national and international communities – by promoting interfaith awareness and campaigns for social justice, such as 'Make Poverty History' and the Fair Trade movement;
- the wider Unitarian community – by bringing like-minded people together, and offering a different model of a Unitarian group.

Miles Howarth says that when we meet, we 'share common experience of a dimension of life that can't be nurtured by other means' (2005). This is the gift of ministry that Unitarians can offer to their communities.

At the heart of Fellowships lie some core values or beliefs. Simply gathering together, being together, and caring for each other engenders a common spirit that nurtures us. The structure of shared Unitarian values holds the group together.

Meeting the stranger

What draws people to join Fellowships? I think it is the basic human need to belong, to come together with like-minded people; and the opportunity to take part in a variety of events or activities, organised by the members themselves: events in which all are included. However, this informal approach does not appeal to everyone. Some people find the openness and freedom, the exposure to different opinions, just too challenging.

I do not think that we should change our approach because of the reaction of a few, but I would add a cautionary note about the group dynamics of Fellowships: 'the moment we begin to bond with a group of like-minded souls, we can set up the dynamics that can result in exclusion and active opposition towards out-groups' (Bloom 2004).

In being together we need to be aware of how our group looks to the newcomer, who may still feel like an outsider, even after many visits. Our hearts and minds may want to convey welcome, outreach, and compassion, and yet our body language and words may give out subtle signals of a well-established, inward-looking group of friends. We need to be open and transparent, and to avoid excluding newcomers by what we choose to talk about. For example, we should avoid discussing committee business or General Assembly matters in front of visitors.

Kay Millard writes that human encounter requires time, effort, commitment, and courage: 'the courage to meet strangers, and open our deep thoughts to them'. When meeting new people, people of other faiths or none, people on spiritual journeys, we will encounter our own doubts, concerns, and even fears. In being conscious of being Unitarian and having responsibilities, we move forward in spite of our doubts and fears.

I am comforted and supported by these words from William Bloom's 'Holistic Creed of Doubt' (2004), which we could offer to visitors to Unitarian groups:

- We celebrate the fact that we may be wrong.
- We warmly welcome opposing views.
- The more different from us you are, the better we like you.
- We trust that the universe is just fine with all this diversity and change.
- These are our beliefs and core values – value them or not.
- We are interested in you, whatever you feel or think about us.

Support for Fellowships

If members address the issue of beliefs and core values soon after a new Fellowship first meets, they will avoid the potential pitfalls created by the lack of a chapel tradition. Fellowships need to form their own tradition and, if naming themselves as Unitarian, need connection with the core values of the Unitarian movement. The Unitarian movement, in turn, needs to seed, nurture, and value all Fellowships.

Commenting on how new Fellowships can best be integrated into the wider movement, The Fellowships Initiative Group (FIG) had this to say:

> While fellowship members without previous contact with the Unitarian movement may well need help and time to explore and grasp fully 'what this thing is that I have joined', they will also be unlikely to accept 'this is the way we always do it', or to have any

reverence for tradition *per se*. The acceptance of the value of any aspect of Unitarian tradition or practice will depend on how they are presented to newcomers and how newcomers perceive them in the light of contemporary realities and their own experience. It may be necessary to help a district association, or others in the denomination, to recognise the validity of new forms so that innovative new fellowships feel welcome and encouraged as truly Unitarian.

FIG (now sadly disbanded) also sought to help new Fellowships to think about the kind of group they wanted to be; for instance:

- A general discussion group, with or without some form of worship. This kind of group might generate topics from its members, or make use of Unitarian religious education materials for adults, or both.
- A Unitarian group that gathers for worship as well as fellowship.
- A group with a Unitarian ethos which has a particular function, such as children's religious education or social action.

However, this does not cover all the possibilities. What about a not-on-Sunday group? Alternatively, what about organising social activities before or after a Fellowship meeting: cinema, theatre, coffee shop, or pub get-together? The answer must surely be based on members' interests. In the words of Fellowship member Kath Mayor, *'Do we work with the people we've got, or a hypothetical Sunday group?'*

Suggestions for future growth

Kay Millard writes that 'the ideal Unitarian Fellowship is an enabling group' (Millard 2002); but first a fellowship needs to *be* enabled. In conclusion, I offer some suggestions that might benefit both congregations and Fellowships:

- Congregations could seed new Fellowships, offering different activities on different days of the week.
- Committed Unitarians could establish Fellowships in areas where there are no churches currently. There should be a Unitarian presence in every major population centre, whatever name the group uses.
- Publicity on the Internet is needed.
- The National Unitarian Fellowship (NUF) could connect members living in the same areas, in order to start new Fellowships.
- Leadership could be provided by lay volunteers, lay leaders, or ministers.
- Fellowship members could be trained to conduct rites of passage and offer this service to the wider community. (Registrars are starting to fill a noticeable gap in this respect.)
- Ministerial or lay-leader oversight is valuable during times of growth, supporting the strategic planning of activities, and helping to organise informal pastoral care. This is a model of facilitation (not leadership) that needs to be developed.
- Short courses on pastoral care might be opened to Fellowship members.
- Funding is needed – whether from trusts, General Assembly or District funds, congregations or generous individuals – to seed the growth of Fellowships.
- Unitarians who understand the dynamics of establishing and consolidating groups could produce start-up packs for Fellowships.
- Facilitation days for Fellowships and congregations should be arranged, to enable groups to meet and to inspire each other.

Let us be aware of our strengths. We have caring, supportive, committed groups of people who value fellow members and visitors ... who have a sense of togetherness, serving members and the wider community in which the Fellowship is based ... who are outward-looking ...who possess and share Unitarian values ... who value remote communication through websites, e-mail, newsletters, and by telephone, as well as meeting face to face ... who can offer pastoral care informally, yet with sensitivity ... who enjoy shared meals (which offer a valuable community experience, especially for people who live alone) ... who enjoy a wide range of shared activities, and even the planning of them!

A useful exercise is to take a strategic view of the future of your group by drawing an imaginary line on the floor and moving forward five, ten, and then twenty years in the future. Participants are asked to think positively about what activities they can imagine their group doing at that point in time. Then they can develop a plan for bringing those ideas into reality – from the present, one step at a time.

In my opinion, as a Unitarian of only a few years' standing, Unitarians are probably the best-placed community of faith in the present century to meet the spiritual needs of those seeking a non-dogmatic, safe space in which to explore their spirituality or individual theology. As a movement we must seize the opportunities of this time, to share fellowship with other spiritual travellers, choosing the path of courage and openness – embracing the change that new ways of being together with new people will bring.

References

Bloom, William (2004) *Soulution: The Holistic Manifesto*, London: Hay House

Fellowships Initiative Group (FIG) 'Background paper', no date, London, Development Committee of the General Assembly

Howarth, Miles (2005) Personal communication

Jung, C.G. (1933) *Modern Man in Search of a Soul*, published in translation by Routledge & Kegan Paul; republished by Harvest Books in 1955

Millard, Kay (2002) 'Unitarian Fellowships and the development of community' in *Prospects for the Unitarian Movement*, London: Lindsey Press

Powell, Timothy (2005) Personal communication

The author

Karen Hanley is a Unitarian lay preacher, a past Chair of Unitarian Experience Week, and previously a co-facilitator of Bath Unitarian Fellowship's Spirituality Group. She is a professional facilitator, she runs trainer-facilitator programmes with the Life Academy, and she is an Associate Fellow of the Pre-Retirement Association. Karen also has management experience of the voluntary sector and finance industry. She supports the Fair Trade movement and 'living lightly' in a world that she hopes will be one large, abundant, and connected community.

Questions for reflection and discussion

1. Are Fellowships important because they offer something different from churches, or simply because they plug the geographical gaps in Unitarian coverage across the country?

2. Why might Fellowships be able to attract individuals who are resistant to attending church worship?

3. Is it equally true that Fellowships may be off-putting for some? If so, why do you think that is?

4. Which of the author's 'suggestions for future growth' are likely to prove most useful?

16 The value of retreats for Unitarians

David Monk

Those who meet together in supra-conceptual silence know each other.
(Father William Johnston)

A Buddhist friend told me of an experience when he spent several weeks on a Zen retreat, during which the retreatants sat in silence in the meditation hall every day. For the whole period of the retreat, he sat facing a woman whom he had never met before. When they left the meditation hall each day, there was no socialising of the type that consists of *'Where do you come from?', 'What sort of work do you do?', 'Are you married?', 'Have you any children?', 'That's an attractive jacket you're wearing'*, etc. For the whole of the retreat there was no spoken communication between the woman and himself; but when it came to an end, he felt he knew her more deeply and intimately than he knew members of his immediate family and long-standing friends.

What does it mean to 'retreat'? Many think of it as distancing and withdrawal, during which one has nothing to do with anything or anybody. In fact, it is just the opposite. It is the practice of standing back from all the ego-based attachments that pull us away from who we truly are, so that our awareness is liberated to see things as they are. This is what Buddha meant by the term 'enlightenment'. But I can only see things as they are when I can see myself as I am. When I open my awareness to everything in me, without clinging and aversion, freed from all the conditioning influences that have created the

121

structure of my self-identity from the moment I was born, I see myself as I am, other people as they are, and the world as it is, with unclouded vision. To retreat, then, is to engage in practices that help us to discover who we are, to own and accept who we are. In so doing, we learn to see other people as they are, accept them with compassion, and hence relate to them at a much deeper level.

A retreat does not have to be a period of total silence, although times of silence are an important element, for the reasons given above. It may include singing, dancing, and talking together; addresses on subjects related to the process of deepening our awareness of ourselves and others and the world in which we live, followed by questions and discussion; going for a walk in the countryside (alone or with others); and visiting the local pub in the evening. The essential thing, whatever the retreat programme includes, is to develop a sense of togetherness in everything that we do.

The Meditational Fellowship

I founded a retreat organisation in 1985, called The Meditational Fellowship (TMF), which attracts people with spiritual and/or contemplative interests. Its residential weekends, held in spring, summer, and autumn each year, are very well attended. It was originally intended solely for Unitarians, but several people from outside our movement now attend regularly. At each weekend the programme contains a variety of sessions, led by experienced members of the Fellowship. They include guidance in meditation practices which help to develop concentration and insight, using techniques from a range of spiritual traditions ... periods of silent meditation ... guided meditations ... talks on subjects related to the practice of meditation, usually followed by questions and discussion ...and sessions of movement, chant, and meditative dance.

Some of the sessions are designed to help participants to relax and find spiritual refreshment and renewal through concentrative meditation. Other sessions focus on deepening insight into oneself and increasing awareness of others, a process which sometimes can be quite challenging. Personal support and guidance, therefore, is always on hand throughout the retreat. Participants are invited to use the retreat in whatever way they feel is most helpful to themselves, with no pressure to attend all the sessions. As the weekend proceeds, there is a very noticeable and growing sense of togetherness. Participants arrive on the Friday, often feeling stressed by the pressures of daily life, and leave on the Sunday refreshed, regenerated, and often greatly inspired by the experiences of the weekend, which have brought them together in love; and we each take this sense of deepened connection and togetherness away from the retreat into our congregational, personal, professional, and social relationships.

A popular venue for TMF retreats is The Nightingale Centre at Great Hucklow. People come from as far away as Scotland and the south coast of England. One of the fruits of TMF for the Unitarian movement is that it has generated the formation of meditation groups in churches and chapels around the country, and has fostered links between individual Unitarians around the UK.

Unitarian spirituality

Spirituality has received little attention in the Unitarian movement until recent times. Since the seventeenth century, the main emphasis in our tradition has been on 'rational dissent' – a concern which is not to be despised, because what we call liberal religion is founded on freedom from the dogmas imposed by ecclesiastical authorities, and the empowerment of ordinary people to follow their own consciences and believe what they feel led to believe from within themselves. But some Unitarians see this trend as having produced too strong an emphasis on intellectualism, with a corresponding low profile for spirituality. Since the latter part of the twentieth century, however, there has been a growth of interest in spirituality, reflecting a general trend throughout society: people who have no connection with formal religion are joining various types of spirituality group in their search for the meaning of their existence.

Retreats are environments for exploring and cultivating spirituality. This is a word that can mean different things to different people; but it contains a common essence in all the religious traditions in the world, which I understand as a disposition towards a belief in a transcendent domain of reality, immanent within our temporal human form, which, when consciously realised, produces a sense of interconnectedness with all other sentient beings and the experience of union with the Unmanifest, or Ultimate Being, commonly referred to as God. All the traditions define the sense of separateness arising from attachment to our self-concept or ego-structure as an illusion. Spiritual practices the world over are designed to help us to break free from the prison of separateness and find union with Ultimate Being. A lovely expression for this is found in the *Mundaka Upanishad* in the Indian tradition:

> As rivers flowing into the ocean find their final peace, and their name and form disappear, even so the wise become free from name and form and enter into the radiance of the Supreme Spirit. (Mascaro 1973)

To retreat, in the true sense, is to engage in spiritual practices. TMF retreats include such from many world traditions. We sit in silence, following the breath, silently repeating a mantra, letting our eyes rest on a candle flame, or bringing an image to mind behind closed eyes. This is silent concentrative meditation. We do guided meditations in which we start by focusing on sensations in the body and then observe the mental images, feelings, emotions, and memories that rise into consciousness in association with these sensations. There is a whole range of practices like this, which are called 'insight meditation'. We also chant and dance together, drawing on traditions across the world, and we practise Tai Chi and Qi Gung exercises. There is also time for talk and discussion. Someone may give an address on Buddhist practice, or the teachings of Lao Tzu, or St John of the Cross, for example; and this is followed by questions and discussion, and then concluded usually with a period of silence and/or a chant. These practices of silent sitting, self-exploration, singing, movement, and group discussion help us to know each other more deeply and intimately. They increase our sense of Oneness. This is spiritual practice, which certainly leads us to that place of 'Being Together'.

Other forms of retreat

The Nightingale Centre, of course, is used for all sorts of Unitarian events, such as Religious Education Summer School, Experience Week, Walking Weekends, and other types of Unitarian conference and workshop, when people throughout the Unitarian movement come together from all over the country. It is also hired from time to time for congregational weekends, when members of a church are resident together for a weekend or few days of activity (for example, to celebrate their church anniversary), or for a period of rest, which they see as a retreat. Their experience of 'being together' in this way is often quite different from what they experience in midweek groups, committee meetings, and Sunday attendance at their local church. Such events are ways of bringing people together from the same congregation in a different way, and introducing and forming fellowship links between people from congregations throughout the UK. The effect is that members of a congregation from the same church get to know each other better, and members of congregations from different parts of the country strengthen their connection with fellow Unitarians nationally.

I feel strongly that retreats are a valuable resource for strengthening and developing our Unitarian movement, by attracting people who are searching for a spiritual environment in which they feel free to be who they are and enter deeply into fellowship with others of a similar mind. I feel also that they have the effect of raising the quality of fellowship within and between congregations.

Reference

Mascaro, J. (1973): *The Upanishads*, p. 81, Penguin Classics

The author

Revd David Monk ministers at the Unitarian Chapel in Hindley near Wigan. In addition to his chapel commitments, he spent several years working as a tutor in pastoral counselling and spiritual practice at Unitarian College Manchester, and as a counselling tutor in higher education. He is the leader of The Meditational Fellowship, runs workshops on meditation with Unitarian groups around the country, and contributes regular articles on the theory and practice of meditation to *Faith and Freedom*. One of his main interests is the parallels between psychotherapy and the contemplative practices of the world's religions.

Questions for reflection and discussion

1. Are you personally attracted to residential retreats of the type outlined above, or not? Let your responses be honest, identifying those elements that attract you, and those that do not.

2. How can those who take part in residential events share the benefits with those unable to attend?

3. Is there some other type of residential activity that you feel would be more helpful to yourself and fellow Unitarians generally?

4. Do you think an increasing emphasis on spiritual practices will help Unitarians generally to strengthen congregational life and attract people to the Unitarian movement?

17 The National Unitarian Fellowship: present reality, future possibilities

Joan Wilkinson

The National Unitarian Fellowship (NUF) is a postal and e-mail fellowship consisting of about 275 members, most living in the UK, but supplemented by a small and growing number of members in other countries. It was founded in 1945 'to provide a channel of communication between people who value a free and positive approach to religion, without dogmatic limits to the individual's quest for spiritual truth' (in the words of the Constitution of the National Unitarian Fellowship). Its purpose remains unchanged, sixty years later.

The founders of the Fellowship aimed to develop channels of communication between members through correspondence and a regular newsletter, and to put isolated members in touch with one another or with a suitable organisation where they might find a basis for fellowship. They also encouraged the formation of groups for study and/or worship. Publicity and outreach was a central focus from the outset. Full co-operation with like-minded organisations was encouraged.

Since its foundation, the NUF has developed a programme of outreach to members of individual Unitarian congregations and fellowships, to those who can no longer attend church (either through illness or through geographical isolation), and to a growing number who have chosen to identify with other Unitarians without feeling the need to congregate in a specific church or chapel. This diversity is reflected in the composition of the Committee and the voluntary helpers who are responsible for the organisation and administration of the Fellowship: out of twenty who are directly active in ensuring the smooth running of the NUF, twelve are members of Unitarian congregations (four of that number being ministers), and the remaining eight are Unitarian by way of belonging only to the NUF. No one is considered to be 'more Unitarian' than another, in a non-hierarchical organisation which functions purely through the goodwill of all its members, there being no paid officers.

What is a congregation?

This unique Unitarian organisation, within the larger Unitarian family, challenges us to consider what we mean by the term 'congregation' – for its members rarely congregate. Meeting together takes place not face to face but through the written word in the monthly publications and within small letter-writing fellowships; or in the virtual world of the Internet, where on-line sermons and prayers, small e-mail fellowships, and an e-mail forum are creating new opportunities for members to explore what it means to experience, build, and be part of a religious community in the twenty-first century. (The website address is www.nufonline.co.uk.)

For the purposes of this essay, a cross-section of NUF members was asked the question *'In what ways is the NUF a congregation?'* Their responses echoed those of a smaller group of NUF members, who, in 2002, addressed the question *'What is community, and how does it relate to place?'* as part of an MA study conducted by NUF member Melanie Prideaux. The study concluded that both 'community' and 'congregation' are terms that are given meaning by the people using them. The responses of the larger group, who contributed their ideas for this present essay, confirmed the conclusions reached by Melanie Prideaux: the multi-faceted nature of this unique organisation allows and encourages its members to define and give meaning to the Fellowship.

Almost all of those who responded to the question, 'In what ways is the NUF a congregation?' felt that the NUF was a congregation *'in the sense that we are a gathering together of minds'*. Members appreciate the quality of engagement and exchange of ideas, which for them can often be more nourishing than the interactions in a typical congregation. For some members, the opportunity to talk 'on-line' can be easier than meeting face to face; for some, such exchanges are vital for their spiritual health. One member in Sweden said that for her it did not matter that in a geographical sense she lives farthest away of all the e-fellowship members, because she can be very near via her computer, and without this communication with other NUF members she could not really call herself a Unitarian.

Some members feel that the NUF is in fact the largest of Unitarian congregations, a fact which gives them access to other people with whom they can discuss matters of faith in a way that might not be encouraged within their own local community. A current member joined the NUF specifically in order to participate in one of the small letter-writing fellowships, where she could have a safe space, without rules and regulations, in which to work out her ideas with others in a spirit of reason, freedom, and tolerance. It was the opportunity to exchange ideas outside a traditional congregational setting that appealed to her. There is an overwhelming consensus that the NUF should not be compared with other congregations and should never be thought of as 'second best'. In some ways it is an ideal congregation for many people living in a society that is increasingly mobile, with working patterns that are very different from what has gone before. While new members are welcomed and given every opportunity to extend their contribution to the NUF and the wider Unitarian family, if they choose to stay only for a short while, they can leave without any fuss or pressure.

It should be acknowledged, however, that the replies quoted above were mostly from members who are active within the smaller fellowships. There were some who felt that without the element of meeting together for worship we are definitely not a congregation, but rather an organisation which facilitates networking between Unitarians from the many independent Unitarian congregations throughout the UK. One member said that she appreciated *'...contact with like-minded folk all over the country. Unitarians being thin on the ground, this was necessary so as not to feel alone in one's ideas and questions.'*

A time of transition and transformation

The NUF is a diverse and many-faceted religious community. The numerical size and spread of the organisation, with its fluid boundaries and its unique and coherent identity, places the Fellowship in an ideal position to be creative when considering future possibilities. There are three distinct aspects that must be taken into account. Firstly, the development of opportunities within the Fellowship. Secondly, the development of a sense of belonging to the whole Unitarian family through the General Assembly and beyond. And finally, developing opportunities for members of individual congregations to engage with other Unitarians beyond their own community.

The impact of the Internet

The first fifty years of the NUF established a religious community based on communication via the written word: postal correspondence between members in several small groups and the distribution of good-quality publications were at the heart of the Fellowship. However, the past ten years have demonstrated that this well-established model is ideally placed to embrace and develop the opportunities provided by the Internet. It was only as recently as 1997 that a few members recognised the value of e-mail communication, and not until the NUF website was launched in 1998 that full advantage could be taken of this new medium. Members and non-members alike appreciate the growing volume of material available to them, which includes the text of a weekly meditation; a worship page specifically created for Unitarians who do not meet at church; video clips presenting statements of faith; and comprehensive material on various aspects of the Fellowship, past and present.

Based on the model of the small letter-writing fellowships, the new small e-mail fellowships are already indicating the possibilities for extending this model to develop interest groups within the larger NUF. Space could easily be made available on the NUF website for future groups to develop a means of networking within the Fellowship and beyond. The Internet also offers an opportunity to provide communication and networking between children, youth, and young adults. The possibilities for both NUF and younger Unitarians could be very exciting.

However, the enthusiasm for developing the potential of the Internet must not undermine the continuing importance of NUF publications. Rather, electronic communications should complement printed publications. Increased e-mail activity is already highlighting the many and varied creative talents within the membership, almost all of whom have been attracted to the NUF through a love of the written word as central to their spiritual life. Initial fears that the Internet would undermine the NUF are now seen to be unfounded, as many of the electronic discussions are based on printed Unitarian publications – books, articles, and sermons – read and circulated within Unitarian circles; such discussions are prompting suggestions for new published material. What both the Internet and the written publications offer the member-ship, as well as interested enquirers, is a safe place to be creative, to engage with and develop new ideas. The Fellowship must not allow the development of its printed publications to lag behind that of the Internet, because the possibilities for increasingly sophisticated printed material are being developed all the time.

A community within a community

With the extra opportunities offered by the Internet, the time has arrived to achieve a greater integration with the wider Unitarian family through the General Assembly and beyond. Although this process already takes place at a modest level, it has become clear that far more could be achieved by increased linking of websites and offering space on the NUF website to various interest-groups already in existence outside the Fellowship. Efforts are already being made on the website to advise members of national and local events, but a greater impact could be made, and more NUF members reached, if a specific message board was made available and used by Unitarian organisations to advertise their programmes of events and communicate other information that might be of interest to NUF members. There are also possibilities to be explored in networking with international organisations such as the International Council of Unitarians and Universalists. The early Internet experience has already indicated the fluidity of the NUF's boundaries, with an increasing number of enquirers from abroad, some who maintain a continuing e-mail contact with the Fellowship and some who are directed elsewhere. The Fellowship is particularly well placed to develop international links.

NUF members need to be aware of the possibilities beyond their own Fellowship, in order to make a meaningful contribution to the future of Unitarianism in the wider sphere. Although many members read the long-established national Unitarian publications, *The Inquirer* and *The Unitarian*, many do not, so we need to explore ways of including NUF members in the wider Unitarian family, in the same way that these publications give a sense of belonging to current readers. It is interesting to speculate whether in time these publications will be available on the Internet.

Finally, ways must be explored of developing opportunities for members of individual congregations to engage with other Unitarians through the NUF, beyond the limitations of any one congregation. The membership of the NUF, with its growing number of internal smaller fellowships, is larger than any one congregation and therefore offers a wider resource on which individuals could draw. One member commented that the NUF might become an organisation of *'communities within the Unitarian community'*. Along with a continuing effort to develop an integrative role for the NUF within the Unitarian movement in this country, there are real possibilities for adding vitality to the NUF, individual congregations, and the wider Unitarian family. The NUF could well prove to be a crucial point of outreach, development, and growth not only for its own members, but also for the wider Unitarian community.

Sources and references

Prideaux, M. (2002) 'What is community, and how does it relate to place?' www.nufonline.co.uk, last checked by the author in December 2004

National Unitarian Fellowship (2005) 'Aims', *Viewpoint for the Jubilee*, Issue 179, February 2005

About the author

Before retirement Joan Wilkinson worked in community and college settings, supporting individual students and establishing self-advocacy groups for adults experiencing difficulties that included homelessness, learning difficulties, mental health problems, head injury, and terminal illness. Her long-term studies with the Open University enabled her to pilot and introduce its distance-learning courses for adults with learning difficulties. This experience of distance learning helped her to appreciate fully the benefits that the National Unitarian Fellowship offers. She regards the opportunity to serve as Secretary to the NUF as a great privilege.

Questions for reflection and discussion

1. Is the purpose for which the NUF was established sixty years ago still relevant today?

2. Is the voluntary nature of its organisation adequate to fulfil the potential of the NUF?

3. Should the NUF operate as a support to existing congregations and fellowships. If so, how?

4. What options might be developed to increase the scope for NUF members to keep in touch with each other and get more involved in the wider Unitarian community?

Part Four
Growing congregations

18 New building – new hope

Vernon Marshall

On Easter Sunday 2003, with a great sense of pride and joy, I stepped into the pulpit to conduct the very first service in the New Chapel, Denton. In December 2002 the congregation of the Wilton Street Chapel had witnessed the closure of their much-loved building to make way for a new shopping precinct. There were mixed feelings: happy memories were associated with the old building, but the deterioration of the area had created an unhappy environment in which to house a congregation. As the members arrived for their first service in the new building, there was a palpable feeling of hope and joy – a feeling that has not gone away.

Since that first service in 2003, I have had time to reflect on the tremendous privilege of ministering in such a new building. It is not the first time that I have ministered in a modern building. The Croydon congregation meets in a 1959 structure, and the Birmingham New Meeting Church was built only in 1973. The experience of ministering in these buildings contrasted greatly with my experiences in Scarborough (built 1877), Whitby (1750), the old Denton building, Wilton Street Chapel (1879), and the locus of my other current ministry: the Old Chapel in Dukinfield (1840). The difference between the New Chapel in Denton and the Croydon building, however, is the latter's almost utilitarian feel, which is due to the fact that its design was determined by the limited resources made available by the government to replace the former building, destroyed during World War II. The New Meeting Church in Birmingham is a beautiful building that does not, surprisingly, contain a dual-purpose working space. This has meant the existence of a room specifically intended for worship, which has retained some elements of a traditional arrangement. Also, in none of these examples was I the first to minister in the new building. To preach the very first service in the New Chapel, Denton, then, was a unique experience for me.

The first notable feature of the new building is the light that fills it. With its numerous and large windows, there is a constant supply of light during the daytime, with adjustable ambient lighting for the evenings. The dominance of natural light is a feature that serves as an admirable metaphor for the theological position of the chapel. The mission of any Unitarian congregation is to bring the light of reason and self-discovery into the dark places of our lives. We celebrate what is natural, and we eschew the hidden meanings that are bound up in the mysterious. When the sun breaks through the clouds on a Sunday morning, and light cascades through the stained-glass window above the pulpit, allowing various colours to dance upon the chapel floor, then the prayers of praise to the wonder of life really do come alive.

The need for continuity

The stained glass at Denton is an example of a feature that in my view should characterise new chapel buildings. Although a new building should be bold and reflect the architectural tradition of the times, it should also contain something of the past. To build something completely devoid of connections with the past would break the hearts of its members, as did the banal structure that replaced the Solomonic Temple of Jerusalem and caused the old men to shed tears (Ezra 3:12). New Chapel may be a new building, but it is not a new congregation. The stained-glass window that is such a focal point of the New Chapel was an integral part of the old Wilton

Street Chapel. Situated at the back of the building, however, it was barely noticed and in no position to be loved as it is now. Pictures, plaques, and the sanctuary furniture were brought from the old building, the reading desk that is now used as a pulpit having at one time been a feature of the Mottram congregation. Thus the new encapsulates the old, and there is a sense of continuity, a connection with the past that points us to the future.

A flexible structure

A feature of most modern church architecture is the practical nature of the building. The more modest size and the low ceiling mean that utility charges are much reduced, and the congregation can thus focus on matters other than the management of the property. Furthermore, New Chapel, Denton is greatly appreciated by funeral directors because of the ease and dignity with which funerals can be performed. There are no steps to climb, the doorways are wide, and the chapel doors are high enough not to knock off the flower arrangements that usually sit on the top of a coffin. The cortege can proceed to the front of the chapel without awkward manoeuvres because, in the absence of fixed pews, sufficient space can easily be made available.

A hallmark of the New Chapel design is its simplicity. Within that simplicity, however, there is beauty: the edifice is neither bland nor bare. Its simplicity has a major advantage in that neither the architecture nor the furniture dictates the theological basis of worship life. Colleagues will know just how difficult it is to explain the non-dogmatic nature of our faith to a newcomer when surrounded by prominent plaques bearing the Ten Commandments, or injunctions that warn 'Prepare to meet thy God'. There may be stained-glass windows that, though beautiful, nonetheless reflect those found in the cathedrals of the mainstream form of religion that we are glad to have left behind. Fixed pews and a high pulpit oblige the congregation to worship in a form that is suggestive of the 'transcendent theology' (McIntyre 1983:577) of the nineteenth century. Movable furniture allows for worship in the round, or in rows facing each other in 'antiphonal' style, reflecting the more modern concept of the 'immanence' of the Divine (*ibid.*: 287). A modern structure reflects a modern outlook on life and religion, and thus gives a positive message to the local community.

New building, new life

As the different impositions of the architecture mean that activities have to be conducted differently, there is tremendous potential for trying out something new. I have encountered a greater willingness to experiment than was ever the case with the old building. The different situation suggests a new start, a recognition that an old practice and a new building make a poor marriage. The congregation of New Chapel was itself looking for something new and different. This places a tremendous responsibility on the minister's shoulders, however. If a desirable change is not initiated at the beginning of the life of the new building, then it is much harder to achieve when the building is no longer new. New Chapel, Denton has initiated many new features in its worship. There have been services to mark the changing seasons (Marshall 2004a), experimental 'communion' services, meditations, and worship that uses elements which avoid the formal, patriarchal language of traditional Unitarian Christianity (Marshall 2004b). All of these changes would have been impractical in the traditional format of the old building. Not one single member has felt alienated by the changes. On the contrary, attendances have almost doubled since 1999, and several new attenders have become formal members.

Private space and public space

One aspect of chapel life that is important to the membership is the use of the building as a community resource. With the dual-purpose nature of the main room, the provision of a modern kitchen, and the spacious storage facilities, the building is an attractive venue for letting to local organis- ations. The ability to shut away the 'sanctuary' area means that there is a small space that is sacrosanct, our own private sacred space. The large area that is left can be used for almost any purpose and is not dominated by religious symbols that could scare away some groups. Paradoxically, the screening of the sanctuary means that visiting organisations are brought right in to the very heart of the chapel, the space where the worshipping life of the congregation takes place. There is also something inexplicably satisfying about the enjoyment of social activities taking place in the same space as worship; the design of the chapel makes a physical statement that devotion and fun are both integral to chapel life.

From my two-year experience of ministering in a new building, I can only confirm our aspirations that were expressed when the chapel was merely an idea in an architect's head. The congregation believed that a new building could presage a new start. Planning a new base did, without my prompting, encourage Denton Unitarians to reflect on where they were currently, and where they wanted to go, in both theological and practical terms. There is now a sense of commitment and drive that did not seem to be present with the same intensity before. New Chapel, Denton is full of hope. Challenges are always presenting themselves, but the members are not deterred. With gratitude for its past, and a firm eye on the future, New Chapel, Denton is happily carrying out its mission with a devotion propelled by a hope that was ignited by its new and beautiful premises.

Sources and references

MacQuarrie, J. (1983) 'Immanentism', *A New Dictionary of Christian Theology*, London: SCM

Marshall, V. (1990) 'Building on the past', *NUF Viewpoint*, no. 94, October 1990

Marshall, V. (2000) 'New beginnings in Denton', *The Inquirer*, 15 July 2000

Marshall, V. (2003) 'Profile of New Chapel, Denton', *The Unitarian*, no. 1192, May 2003

Marshall, V. (2004a) 'A happy Sunfest to you all', *Unitarian Earth-Spirit Network File*, no. 25, Summer 2004

Marshall, V. (2004b) *In Praise of the Mystic Dancer*, Manchester: Provincial Assembly of Lancashire and Cheshire

McIntyre, J. (1983) 'Transcendence', *A New Dictionary of Christian Theology*, London: SCM

The author

Vernon Marshall became a Unitarian Lay Pastor in 1981 and a recognised Minister in 1985. He has ministered to congregations in Scarborough, Whitby, Birmingham, and Croydon and now serves the Old Chapel, Dukinfield and the New Chapel, Denton, both of which are in Greater Manchester. He has qualifications from the Universities of Leeds, Manchester, London, Birmingham, and the Open University and has recently completed a doctoral programme with the University of Derby.

Questions for reflection and discussion

1. How can a congregation find ways to agree on what shape and style a new church building should be?

2. What are the features of any new church building that could most fully represent modern Unitarianism?

3. How true is it that modern church buildings are efficient on practical grounds but aesthetically unpleasing?

4. How can a new church building connect with the traditions of its Unitarian past?

5. What are the disadvantages of worshipping in a new building?

19 Should congregations set themselves goals?

Tony Cann

In our own way, we are setting ourselves personal goals the whole time. We plan our lives through our diaries and by other means. Without such plans, we would not achieve much in our lives. For example, we would probably not go on holiday if we didn't plan to do so. We wouldn't save for it. We wouldn't book it. We wouldn't prepare for it. You cannot decide to go on holiday at an hour's notice (you will probably not get a vacancy). You cannot just wake up one morning and run half a marathon (at least I cannot). We need to plan in advance – set our goals.

The same thing applies to groups of people who live, work, and worship together. Families have goals, such as to meet up once a year. If the reunions were not planned in advance, they would never happen. People plan to have enough money for retirement, by saving for many years beforehand. If they didn't, they probably wouldn't be able to lead the sort of life that they would like. Companies set themselves goals, often in relation to budgets. Their goals often concern sales and profits; but a set of subsidiary goals is needed in many areas. Without these goals not only would they lack the focus that directs all their employees, but they might not have the resources in place for the necessary steps to be taken.

So should religious congregations set goals? Is there any evidence that setting goals would help them? You might think that the answer to the first question is a self-evident *yes*. However, let us assume for the time being that it is not self-evident. In any case it cannot be so, because many congregations do not set goals, and we may therefore assume that they don't believe that goals will help them.

What do we mean by 'goals'?

First we need to define what is meant by 'setting goals'. It means deciding to try to reach a particular state or position in the future. We might, for instance, want to increase our church membership, increase our income, hold certain events, or raise money for charity. Without membership we have no community, and without activities we won't have a community either.

Setting goals for a worshipping community is nothing new. We have always decided that we want to do certain things, such as holding special services or organising a Christmas Fair. Some things, however, are not deliberately decided: we simply do them out of habit or custom, year in and year out. Setting goals does not interfere with these activities, but requires the congregation to choose a few special things that they want to focus on in particular over a coming period, whether short or long.

What sorts of goal?

What sorts of goal should be adopted in a congregation? The answer will vary according to the needs and desires of each community. What is important is to limit the number of goals and to choose those that will have the greatest impact. The process of setting goals is not a quick and easy one; to be most effective, it should usually involve thorough discussion.

Setting goals is, in fact, more than identifying a desired outcome: goals are usually framed in a form that can be measured or verified. For instance, rather than stating simply that we wish to increase membership, it is more helpful to quantify the increase that we are aiming to achieve. We do not simply say *'we wish to raise money for charity'*: we need to quantify how much we want to raise. This allows us to be able to say at the end of the period whether or not we have achieved the goals. Some goals, if they cannot be quantified, include a time period in which the goal is to be achieved: for example, an intention to construct a new car park for the chapel by a certain date. Sometimes the goal will not necessarily apply only to one year: we can aim to achieve a goal over a longer period, but we should break down the work involved into steps that cover shorter periods. Generally, to make goals relevant, it is better not to allow too long a time-span.

In choosing a quantity or a time-frame, we need to stretch ourselves and at the same time be realistic. In commercial companies, it is a cynical ploy to choose goals that will be achieved anyway; but in our congregations we need to choose goals that will challenge us, while remaining within the realms of possibility. There is no point in choosing goals that are too easy; but choosing goals that are impossibly ambitious is even worse, because we will tend to become discouraged and give up trying. We should not hesitate to set seemingly modest goals – particularly in terms of increasing membership – because modest increases over several years will eventually accumulate to constitute a substantial increase.

Not all goals are concerned with increasing numbers. We might set a goal of increasing the variety of worship by holding a number of special services, or by organising a meditation group. Or we might set out to create a fuller social life for the congregation by, for instance, holding a concert party once a year.

Why should we set ourselves goals?

Why do this? Firstly, the process of setting goals creates a set of key activities and focuses the congregation's energies on

147

achieving them. Secondly, it creates measures against which the congregation can monitor their progress. Thirdly, it causes the congregation to think about what they want to do. Finally, setting goals causes things to happen that would not otherwise take place.

Congregations are no different from other organisations. They need to decide communally what they want to achieve, so that all members can focus on the task and play a part in reaching their goals. The word 'their' is very important, because a key advantage in setting agreed goals is the fact that the whole community takes ownership of the project and is mobilised towards achieving its aims.

Setting the goals is only a first step. Everybody is then involved, and needs to decide what should be done to achieve the goal. For instance, if the goal is to give a certain amount to charity in the year, some events might need to be organised to raise funds. The congregation that has committed itself to the goal will need to work out how the goal is going to be achieved. Everybody should be kept informed through the newsletter. A greater sense of 'ownership' will be generated in this way. Setting goals can have valuable side effects. When they are achieved, we can celebrate and feel good about ourselves and our community. Without any goals, we lose the opportunity to celebrate.

Two real-life examples

As a result of input some years ago by Charles Gaines, a retired Unitarian Universalist minister, the Unitarian congregation at Padiham in Lancashire set themselves a series of goals, ranging from increasing membership to building a new car park, and including raising money for charity. We managed to achieve most of these goals. The process of annual goal setting has continued, and we can see that we would be lost without it.

The process in Padiham starts with meetings of the chapel committee, where ideas are collected and measures discussed. For instance, the committee considered what we had managed to give to charity in the previous year and set a goal for the coming year. The goals were then presented to the congregation, to be either modified or rejected. In fact none was rejected at this stage, although the measures were modified. Generally the congregation was supportive of the whole exercise, since the goals were self-evidently sensible, and consultation helped everyone to pull together to achieve them. During the year we watched how we were doing. We were not always successful. For instance, we set ourselves a goal of appointing a new minister within a certain time, and the timescale slipped. But the fact that the timescale slipped gave added impetus to our efforts.

There are different ways of setting goals. One method, sometimes called 'appreciative inquiry', is well described in a publication issued by Myrada,[1] an organisation which works with rural communities in India. The groups begin with an appreciation of what is good about the current state of affairs, and move forward to consider where they would like to be in the future. This helps them to identify their goals. Good visions inspire people; they are challenging but achievable; they create tensions between what is currently happening and what the group wants to achieve; and they stir the group to action. Myrada's experience shows that the goals should be specific, measurable, and commensurate with the group's current resources. They should be based on the strength of the group and its past achievements. The group should be willing to adopt new forms of engagement, if required, in order to achieve the goals.

A cause for celebration

I think the majority of members of our congregation at Padiham are aware of most of the goals that were set and have accepted ownership of most of them. Many of our achievements – for example, the task of finding a minister, and the task of raising the £18,000 needed to replace our organ – would not have been achieved without the discipline of setting goals, and the congregation would not have been so actively engaged in reaching them. So yes, goals do help.

If you still need to be convinced, consider trying to make progress in a congregation without a process of setting goals. There will be less commitment to the future; a weaker sense of common cause; less planning; less honest assessment of how well the congregation has done – and less cause for celebration. If agreed goals are set, the congregation will have chosen those that they really are committed to; they will feel a sense of ownership of the resulting projects; and they will have been actively engaged in the planning. Ultimately they will have faced up to the fact that some have not been achieved; they will have worked out a plan to do better in the future; and they will have great cause for celebration when their main goals are achieved.

Notes

The Positive Path – Using Appreciative Inquiry in Rural Communities, by Graham Ashford and Saleela Patkar, 2001. Can be downloaded free from www.iisd.org/ai/myrada.htm.

The author

Tony Cann was the son of an Austrian refugee Jewish father and a Catholic mother. At University in Manchester he organised student help in local youth clubs and was influenced by helpers who were training for the Unitarian ministry. Later he joined Padiham Nazareth Chapel and was its Secretary for several years. He is also a member of the Committee of Unitarian College, Manchester and has served as its Secretary for a number of years. Tony is a Trustee of the Hibbert Trust and currently its Chair. Recently he was a founder member of the Renaissance Group and a member of the Governance Task Force.

Questions for reflection and discussion

1. What's wrong with congregations just carrying on as they have always done?

2. Has your congregation worked out specific goals to achieve? How were they decided upon?

3. Does goal setting require a certain discipline which Unitarian congregations find hard to live by?

4. Is goal setting compatible with the spiritual purpose of a congregation?

20 The benefits of congregational consultancy

Don Phillips and Linda Phillips

The idea of congregational consultancy in the Unitarian movement began with the creation of the Small Congregations Consultancy Panel in 2000. It was inspired by Revd Keith Gilley, who, during his term of service as President of the General Assembly, had identified a great need to intervene to re-energise the smallest congregations in the movement. 'Small', in this context, meant those congregations that felt they could no longer achieve growth and development through their own resources, but did have sufficient numbers to stand a good chance of becoming self-sufficient after an appropriate short-term programme of support.

The Panel consisted of representatives of the General Assembly committees as they were constituted at the time. With support from the Unitarian Millennium Fund, the Panel appointed us, the authors of this chapter, as its professional consultants. Our remit was to design and implement a process that would facilitate two things: the analysis of small congregations that aspired to grow, and the initiation and fulfilment of developmental projects that were within those congregations' limited resources – with District support as appropriate.

The aim: helping congregations to help themselves

The Small Congregations Consultancy Panel completed its work in 2003, after we had worked with ten 'client' congregations, with varying degrees of success. Success was largely dependent upon the extent to which a congregation had already declined to a level that made any sustained effort too difficult for its remaining members. Even had such a decline not taken place, congregations needed to be willing to contemplate change, and to pick themselves up by their boot straps. Some congregations did achieve sustainable growth – a growth that was enabled by the consultancy process, but resulted primarily from the members' own renewed enthusiasm, energy, and commitment. The project's aim was not to do the work *for* the congregations, but to facilitate their own efforts and help them to achieve their potential. As outsiders, we could only enable the members of a congregation to help themselves; sustained energy had to be supplied by the congregation. The fruits of the process are still being realised, and only time will tell the true long-term benefits.

The process was judged successful, and both the Panel and the General Assembly believed that the techniques that it had employed should be made available, in the longer term, to enable congregations of any size to benefit from the process. Indeed, by involving larger and more resourceful congregations, success in enabling real and sustainable growth seemed more likely.

Renamed the 'Congregational Consultancy Panel', the Panel conducted a series of regional workshops in 2004 to acquaint representatives of congregations with the project's methodology. The workshops were followed by a two-day seminar in early 2005 to train a team of regionally based volunteer facilitators. This was the final phase of the project that had been supported by the Unitarian Millennium Fund. The trained volunteer facilitators are now licensed by the General Assembly to work through the process with congregations from which they feel a sufficient distance to act as impartial facilitators (for example, not their own congregation), so that the process is no longer reliant on its professional consultants.

Also the work of the Panel has now ended, and responsibility for managing the process has formally passed to the Denominational Support Commission.

Although designed by us, the congregational consultancy process is the copyright of The General Assembly of Unitarian and Free Christian Churches, which licenses its use by the volunteer facilitators, case by case. The process is based on organisation development (OD) techniques – a set of diagnostic tools originally devised for use in business organisations, which is part of our own professional knowledge base. We are pleased that our business skills have proved transferable to a congregational setting, reflecting the fact that our Unitarian ethical standards have influenced our business dealings.

The theory: organisation development

The phases of an organisation-development intervention process include diagnosis, planning, and evaluation. Richard Beckhard's work, *Organization Development: Strategies and Models* is, arguably, the primary theoretical authority for these techniques of analysis. It states:

> An OD program involves a systematic diagnosis of the
> organization, the development of a strategic plan for
> improvement, and the mobilization of resources to carry out the
> effort. (Beckhard 1969, p.9)

What distinguishes organisation development from other organisational change methodologies is that the process is by its nature 'reflective, self-analytical, self-examining, proactive, diagnostically oriented, and action oriented' (French, Bell, and Zawack 1989, p.11). Organisation development is by no means new, and it has become somewhat discredited in the business world in recent decades, largely because of its use of behavioural science and its failure to recognise certain business needs, as opposed to human needs (Armstrong 1989, p.134). We, however, do not accept that this criticism of organisation-development techniques is relevant to their application in this particular context – i.e. to organisations of people working together for non-business purposes, as worshipping communities. Also, we belong, in any case, to a generation of Human Resources professionals who do still see their work in this field through the lens of the behavioural sciences. At the same time, we seek to apply the highest standards of professional rigour from the business world to our work.

Michael Armstrong says of the application of organisation development that development plans result from 'a systematic analysis and diagnosis of the circumstances', which third parties are often engaged to conduct (Armstrong 1996, p.391). The congregational consultancy process is entirely compliant with this statement: using independent facilitators, it analyses, diagnoses, and identifies development plans.

Notwithstanding the need for consistency in the way in which information is gathered and analysed, the success of the intervention also depends on the process remaining flexible. Each congregation is treated as a distinct community, with its own particular needs and circumstances. The touchstones of the process are responsiveness and flexibility.

The practice: from fact-finding to action-planning

Following our original model, the volunteer facilitators use a standardised format – a 'managed questionnaire' or 'fact-finder' – to ensure that the information gathered is as complete as possible, and consistent with information gathered from other congregations. A 'managed questionnaire' is one that is completed by the facilitator (and not by 'targeted' respondents, as is conventional when questionnaires are used to gather data), as he or she works through the sections and questions with the congregation and, if they have one, with their worship leader. Although the 'managed questionnaire' is simple, and easy to work with, this is not a process that is suitable for a congregation to work through without a facilitator. This is because only an *independent* facilitator can probe beyond the superficial – to identify underlying issues and feelings within the congregation. The follow-up questioning and non-verbal observation is at least as important as the framework of the 'managed questionnaire'. The 'managed questionnaire' format will therefore not be made available to anyone who is not trained in this particular process.

For readers with experience of business audit processes, this description will carry a familiar ring. The process is indeed one that would qualify as 'audit'; but we use the analogy with caution, because this particular process in no way implies judgement. It is simply a thorough process of analysis and information gathering, the results of which are applied only to creating and implementing ideas and initiatives that remain under the congregation's control and help them to fulfil their aspirations.

The process begins with an initial full-day fact-finding meeting between the facilitator and representatives of the congregation. In the cases of the initial ten 'small' congregations, this would often mean the entire congregation. As many members as possible should be encouraged to attend – this is not a job for the management committee alone! This initial meeting will be a hard day's work for everyone involved, so enjoying lunch together is important, to provide both a break for all, and an opportunity for the facilitator to get to know people and observe their interactions outside the formality of the meeting. The meeting is best arranged over a weekend, so that the facilitator can also attend normal Sunday worship: such a key feature of congregational life needs to be observed if the facilitator is to gain a complete picture. Elements covered in the analysis include worship, membership, non-worship activities, governance, finances, buildings, outreach, pastoral care, ministry, and any other information that members of the congregation feel is relevant.

A critical part of the facilitator's technique is what we call 'listening at two levels'. By this we mean understanding the factual answers to specific questions while, at the same time, probing more deeply for messages about the relationship dynamics and constraints within the congregation that lie behind the answers. Using discretion and care, the facilitator can also make observations that seek to corroborate, or otherwise, his or her initial perceptions. Congregations and their worship leaders have frequently commented that this fact-finding process led them to make very significant discoveries about themselves, as a congregation, and about their circumstances.

The facilitator will visit the congregation again to talk them through a number of suggested actions that they might take – and to enable the congregation to adopt or amend the actions, as they feel appropriate. During this part of the process, the congregation and the facilitator will together agree plans and break them down into manageable steps, agree who among the congregation is to 'own' and carry out the tasks, and set timescales for the completion of each task. As well as enabling the congregation to achieve what they set out to do, this gives them a mechanism that they can continue to use long after the facilitator's work with them is done.

During a third and final visit, the facilitator will help the congregation to assess progress on their adopted actions, plan the next steps, and put in place an on-going review process. At this point the congregation will also be asked by the facilitator to provide feedback on their impressions of the whole process.

The role of the District Association

We believe that a representative of the congregation's District Association should be present at each meeting, to enable appropriate District resources to be harnessed in support of actions identified by the process. We cannot emphasise too strongly the importance of recognising from the outset that the facilitator's role is to *facilitate* the process – including the congregation's planning and implementation stages. The facilitator should not remain involved beyond this process and actually 'deliver' outcomes for the congregation.

Another reason for involving the District Association is that some congregations who find it difficult, for whatever reason, to participate in District affairs may become isolated and feel vulnerable, and renewed District engagement with them can help to overcome this isolation. Where the congregation has limited resources and expertise of its own, support from the District Association may well be essential to overall success; but permanent dependence upon the District should be avoided, as should dependence upon the facilitator. The object should always be for the congregation to achieve the highest possible level of self-sufficiency.

A possible next step: Engagement Groups

The already proven short-term advantage of congregational consultancy – even if it is something as simple as increased energy levels and sense of purpose within a congregation – can be the beginning of something much more meaningful and sustainable. Alice Mann writes of worshipping communities having a 'life cycle' in which they move from their formation, through a period of stability, followed by decline and death (Mann 1999, p.9). She argues, however, that at the 'decline' stage renewal, revitalisation, and redevelopment are also possible, and a successful congregational consultancy process might help a congregation to understand its place in this cycle and then progress to apply transformational techniques such as the use of Engagement Groups.

Thandeka (Assistant Professor of Theology and Culture at Meadville/Lombard Theological School in Chicago) tells us that 'Small Group Ministries' – small lay-facilitated groups working within worshipping communities and guided by professional supervision – 'are transforming the religious landscape of Unitarian Universalism in the United States' (Thandeka 2002, p.1). Small Group Ministries are known as 'Engagement Groups' in Britain. Thandeka goes on to argue that they 'have the power to similarly revitalise [British] Unitarian ... churches' and make 'transformation' happen in worshipping communities, whether large or small. One plan to emerge from a congregational consultancy might entail a project to investigate the potential use of Engagement Groups. Such a plan could include a discussion of who might be involved, and what kinds of issue the Engagement Groups might initially address. The actual commencement of one or two such groups might be the project's intended outcome.

We invite our readers to consider the questions that follow this chapter – and ask themselves whether or not they feel that the congregational consultancy process might be of assistance in their own worshipping community. If they wish to take the idea further, their congregation should, either directly or through their District Association, contact the Denominational Support Commission.

Note

The Editor asked for the inclusion of illustrative examples, drawing upon personal experience; but because the details of our consultancy work with particular congregations are confidential, we can only describe our experience in the most general and unattributable terms.

References

Armstrong, M. (1989) *Personnel and the Bottom Line*, London: Chartered Institute of Personnel & Development

Armstrong, M. (1996) *A Handbook of Personnel Management Practice*, London: Kogan Page

Beckhard, R. (1969) *Organization Development: Strategies and Models*, Reading, MA: Addison-Wesley Publishing Company

French, W. L., C.H. Bell, and R. A. Zawacki (1989) *Organization Development: Theory, Practice and Research*. Homewood, IL: Richard D Irwin Inc.

Mann, A. (1999) *Can Our Church Live? Redeveloping Congregations in Decline*, Herndon, VA: The Alban Institute

Thandeka (2002) *Engagement Groups: Bringing Forth the Future from the Past*, 2002 Essex Hall lecture, London: Lindsey Press

The authors

Don Phillips and Linda Phillips each have some thirty years' experience as Personnel/Human Resources professionals, both in large corporate organisations and as independent consultants. Their consultancy business, The Hucklow Consultancy, was engaged by the General Assembly of Unitarian and Free Christian Churches from 2000 to 2005 to deliver the Small Congregations/Congregational Consultancy Projects. Both committed Unitarians, Don and Linda have each undertaken ministry training and joined the Unitarian Ministry during the time-scale covered by these projects.

Questions for reflection and discussion

1. Is 'development' solely concerned with attracting new members – or is it about creating a positive atmosphere, so that current members stay committed and newcomers do not drift away?

2. Do you feel that your congregation has a complete picture of itself and the challenges that it faces?

3. Is there any particular aspect of your congregation's life (such as its finances) that you avoid thinking about? If so, what would help you to come to terms with it?

4. What impact would your congregation's literature have on a casual passer-by or a visitor? Does your congregation portray itself attractively?

5. Do you think your congregation could benefit from the congregational consultancy process?

21 Engagement Groups

Margaret Kirk

At the General Assembly meetings at Sheffield in 2002, the Essex Hall Lecture was entitled 'Engagement Groups: Bringing Forth the Future from the Past'. The lecture generated a great deal of excited response. Many of us who heard it felt strongly that the engagement-group process offered something that we could develop with our congregations, something which might bring us into deeper connection with each other, while at the same time attracting people from outside into our congregational communities. It was the speaker, Thandeka, Associate Professor of Theology and Culture at Meadville/ Lombard Theological School in Chicago, who set our imaginations alight. She described Engagement Groups as 'reverential engagement', 'small group ministry', 'an act of right relationship'. She also claimed that 'reverential engagement' is God's work, which takes us beyond the small group into service for the wider community.[1]

I had been fortunate. The previous summer I had attended the Unitarian Universalist annual meetings in Cleveland, Ohio, and had taken part in a workshop where Revd Calvin Dame, minister of the U U Community Church of Augusta, Maine, was talking about Engagement Groups or, as they are commonly called in the USA, Covenant Groups. For me this was where it all began. Before Thandeka came to speak to us, I was already deeply interested in the concept of engagement and what it might have to offer to our UK Unitarian communities. Both Thandeka and Calvin Dame believe that Engagement Groups have the capacity to deepen the spiritual resources of a congregation and open up a vision of service in which all can participate.

At a London District Provincial Assembly quarterly meeting in 2000, Revd Art Lester claimed that 'church is dead'. I think that Thandeka would not endorse that claim, but she would support the view that something more is needed in our communities to give us deeper spiritual connection: something more than most of our church communities are currently able to offer. Thandeka did not claim Engagement Groups as an alternative model of ministry, intended to replace the more orthodox model – although others have gone on to do so. But she did say that, 'as free religionists, engagement offers a place where different persons, divergent beliefs and dissonant claims meet'.[2] She said that these places offer 'an ethos of trust and safety'; and she drew upon the writings of the Jewish theologian, Martin Buber, in stating her belief that these are places where the 'I – Thou'[3] encounter is experienced, 'where the healing presence of God is felt'.

Engagement Groups in practice

Establishing their reasons for coming together helps people to understand that Engagement Groups have a different purpose from some other groups that gather in our congregations. In Engagement Groups there is an intention to listen and share experience, and a desire to be in deeper connection with one another. While it is true that listening, sharing, and being in deeper connection can be wonderful by-products of our other church groups that meet regularly, often these are no more than brief moments of deeper connection, and they are not given the time and scope that they need in order to develop. The process and the purpose of engagement is *always* to provide space for deeper connection – which becomes a transformative spiritual experience.

Currently nine Unitarian churches in the UK are experimenting with Engagement Groups, and others are considering doing so. Although there is a distinctive framework for an Engagement Group, and most groups have adopted it, there will always be some differences of approach. As Calvin Dame says: 'in small groups, we always do it this way, unless we do it some other way!'[4]

This is the way we went about it in my congregation at York. Groups of between six and 12 people met to share more of themselves with each other, to listen and to be heard, to be in deeper connection, to support each other and to be supported. By January of 2003 we had a pilot up and running: four two-hour sessions, running from March to June. I was really excited. Twelve people came. Each session began with an opening ritual: a few words, a chalice lighting, maybe some music. At the first session a covenant was established, enabling members of the group to decide how they wanted to be in relationship with each other: ground rules such as making every effort to attend; being punctual; respecting confidentiality where appropriate; encouraging and welcoming new members. This was followed by a 'check-in', when the participants introduced themselves and told the others anything about themselves that they wished to share.

The check-in is where the real work of engagement begins: each person speaks, each person is listened to. The check-in allows space for engagement as an activity of speaking, receiving, listening. Thandeka refers to this as a period of 'creative interchange...(producing) appreciative understanding of individual differences (where) individual identities are acknowledged (and) no one has to pretend to be just like everyone else'.[5] The check-in is followed by discussion of a chosen topic, or an activity, or maybe an exploration of issues that have arisen during the check-in itself. The session finishes with a brief 'check-out' and a closing ritual of words or music.

Responses to the pilot sessions

This first experiment with an Engagement Group at York did not suit everyone who attended. We lost two people, and one person who valiantly supported it for four sessions had many reservations. But when we evaluated our pilot and asked people to describe their experience of engagement, the responses convinced us that we had sown the seeds of something that touched people deeply, that was distinctively valuable and needed to be nurtured. So we carried on.

Three people volunteered to be facilitators for two new groups. The first one began in the autumn of 2003 and was called *Spirituality Matters*. We invited people into conversation about those aspects of their lives that could broadly be described as spiritual, focusing on such topics as 'Choice, Chance, and Change'; 'Faith and Forgiveness'; and 'Sin and Spirituality'. The second new group had its first meeting in February 2004. It was entitled *Celebrating Diversity* and was based on the material compiled by the (Unitarian) Sexual Orientation Equality Group, designed to help us to explore the roots of intolerance in ourselves and take part in a celebration of difference. Each group attracted eight participants. Again, we had one or two people who had reservations about their experience of engagement. One group had a shaky beginning, but overcame its problems and continued with sustained commitment. As before, despite some initial fears, most participants were positive. At an evaluation session in July 2004, some members of the two groups, when asked to describe what engagement meant to them, replied as follows:

- *'Truly hearing what others are saying, and truly being heard by them.'*

- *'Intention to be open to the other/Other and myself in a process. On a journey of discovering; making connections however clumsily and it being OK to make some mistakes – we can still pick up and carry on learning.'*

- *'To get to know people, to meet each other, to talk with each other, to do more than just listen to an address in a service, to have space to explore issues and topics in a safe way.'*

- *'For me, engagement is about finding something similar to me in someone else and going on to explore the differences.'*

- *'Engagement means to me a promise towards working together for a creative, constructive, and trustworthy partnership.'*

Some challenges

In North America, where most church communities are much bigger than here in the UK, there is much evidence that Covenant Groups meet the spiritual needs of church members who are drawn to the inclusive liberalism of Unitarian Universalism but feel a need for greater intimacy than a Sunday service can offer. Some of these churches have seen attendance grow, and they attribute that growth to the development of Covenant Groups. Here in the UK, where we have much smaller Unitarian communities and where Engagement Groups are in their infancy, it is too early to assess the contribution that they can make.

Most congregations experimenting with Engagement Groups will encounter challenges that need to be faced. Will groups become so self-absorbed that they lose their connection with the church? If people join from outside the church community, how do they relate to the host church community, if at all? At worst, could Engagement Groups be divisive, encouraging closer relationships between group members while creating a sense of exclusion in those who, for whatever reason, are unable to attend? These are legitimate concerns.

While Engagement Groups provide space for people to share some of their life experience in a supportive, accepting environment, they should remain open to newcomers, and they should serve the community from which they have emerged. This service can take a number of different forms: by organising Sunday worship for a particular occasion, for example, or providing a meal, tidying the church grounds, or providing coffee for a special event. Service of this kind sustains connections with the wider community and offsets the possibility of the group becoming excessively self-absorbed. Where this happens and where, in addition, the activities and aspirations of the group are made public, by announcements at Sunday services and in the local newsletter, there is less likelihood that other members of the congregation will experience them as divisive. Nevertheless, I believe that Engagement Groups challenge us to expand our vision of what we mean by 'spiritual practice'.

Reverential engagement

Over these past three years I believe that our groups at York have come close to what Thandeka called 'reverential engagement', where 'different persons, divergent beliefs and dissonant claims meet'. As well as this, I have seen the spirit of engagement at work in other groups, and have come to believe that these groups offer a spiritual practice which has meaning for people in a way that Sunday morning worship does not. In Art Lester's provocative article, published in *The Inquirer* in February 2000, he argued that the Church is dead but God is not, and he urged:

> What we have to do is listen to the world we live in. Not preach to them; listen. We have to have a hard look at Sundays as the time we practise our rituals... We have to review our ministerial

167

training, to move away from an emphasis upon skilled speakers to one of skilled listeners and facilitators... We have to let rituals evolve that speak to the souls of people passing outside.

Might engagement be one of those evolving rituals that 'speak to the souls of people' both inside and outside our churches? There is some evidence that this is the case. For those of us who believe this to be true, the question is: how do we make our churches more accessible for this kind of spiritual activity? How do we use the space more imaginatively? How do we bring loyal members of our congregations with us in agreeing that if we are to 'speak to the souls of people passing outside' we need to diversify and make our churches and chapels into places of vibrant engagement?

Uniquely, our tradition offers space for spiritual practice that transcends tolerance. It offers space for meeting which is a place of reflection and discovery and continual re-discovery, of truly hearing and truly being heard, a place for transformative theology to break through, so that, as Martin Buber famously said, '*all true living is meeting*'.[6]

Notes

1. *Engagement Groups: Bringing Forth The Future from the Past*, the 2002 Essex Hall Lecture, published by the General Assembly of Unitarian and Free Christian Churches, Essex Hall, London.
2. *Ibid.*
3. Martin Buber: *I and Thou*, 1957, published by Charles Scribner's Sons, New York.
4. *Small Group Ministry Resource Book*, Unitarian Universalist Community Church of Augusta, Maine, prepared by Revd Calvin O. Dame.
5. Essex Hall Lecture 2002, *op. cit.*
6. Buber, *op. cit.*

The author

Margaret Kirk taught English in secondary schools in Bradford and Middlesbrough before training for the Unitarian ministry between 1986 and 1988 at Unitarian College Manchester. She has been minister of St Saviourgate Chapel, York since 1988, with pastoral oversight for the Whitby chapel. She is a member of Engagement Support, which helps congregations to organise and sustain engagement groups, is currently welfare officer for the Ministerial Fellowship, and President of the Yorkshire Unitarian Union.

Questions for reflection and discussion

1. Do you think that an Engagement Group could enrich congregational life for you and for others?

2. What kinds of theme might work best for an Engagement Group?

3. Service to the wider community is a required element within the programme of Engagement Groups. Do you think that this fact might make chapel members in general better disposed towards Engagement Groups? Does it matter what form this service to the community might take?

4. What do you understand by Buber's phrase 'all true living is meeting'?

22 The future of small congregations: a transatlantic view

Jane Dwinell

A familiar problem

Once upon a time, there was a small Unitarian Universalist congregation. At one point their membership had numbered about forty, with twenty or so worshipping in church on Sundays. This congregation had a lovely old building, beautiful stained glass, a terrific organ, and a sanctuary with seating for 125. It felt kind of lonely during worship.

Over the years, the congregation struggled. For a while they would have a minister, but then the money would run out, or the minister would find a more lucrative job with a bigger congregation. Sometimes there was conflict, and a few members would leave in disgust. Gradually, the congregation dwindled away, leaving about 25 on the rolls, and a dozen in church on a good Sunday.

The few survivors met and envisioned a different future for the congregation. They wanted to grow; they wanted to spread the word of liberal religion. They had had enough of trying to afford a full-time minister. They wanted a healthy, strong presence in the community, but they were tired of doing all the work themselves.

A realistic solution

So they chose to hire a church co-ordinator, ten hours a week. The co-ordinator would handle all the loose ends of the work done by the volunteers. The co-ordinator made sure that all was in order for Sunday morning, by working with the organist and the worship leader, and creating the order of service. He picked up the mail and the phone messages, and distributed them to the right people. He made sure the heat was on in cold weather, that the toilets were clean, and there was coffee in the kitchen. He paid the bills (with cheques signed by the treasurer), balanced the cheque book, and created monthly financial reports for the governing Board.

And everybody breathed a sigh of relief. The work was getting done; the congregation was happier, and more welcoming to newcomers. New people became *new people* – interesting, and fun – not solely seen as potential new workers and new pledgers.

After a while, the congregation realised that the co-ordinator couldn't do everything – that they needed some services of a minister. There were elderly members in need of care at the end of life. There were local clergy meetings to attend, and networking to be done to spread the word of Unitarian Universalism. There was much to learn about running a church, leading worship, and providing Sunday School for the children.

So they hired the services of a minister – 25 hours a month. They were clear about what they wanted her to do: lead worship once a month, provide pastoral care, attend governing Board meetings, and do outreach in the community. So she did. And, between the clarity of the congregation, the work done by the co-ordinator, and the work done by the minister, they began to grow ... and grow ... and grow. Word got out that there was a liberal religious home in the area, and that the congregation was doing exciting things, like providing a free Thanksgiving dinner for those who were alone and hungry on the holiday. They were speaking out for justice for same-sex couples. They were providing religious education for the children and a high-quality, meaningful Sunday morning worship service, and they were caring for one another in times of need.

Hidden from the visitors, they also had a balanced budget for the first time in years, and began to increase their pledge base. They invited members to commit themselves in advance to an annual contribution, instead of just hoping that people would donate enough money to keep the place going. They also handled conflict differently now. Instead of allowing a disagreement to turn into an *'I'm right, and you're wrong'* event, with the resulting exodus of at least a half a dozen members and simmering anger for years, conflict was seen as an opportunity to talk things out in a positive way, and to look for the gifts that come with change.

Pretty soon, the fellowship hall was too crowded during the Social Hour after the service. And the hall was not accessible to the members and visitors who used walking frames and wheelchairs to get around. So, emboldened by the new-found strength and energy that came from growth, and the focus provided by the minister and the co-ordinator, the congregation voted to build an extension to their historic church building – an addition that would be accessible to all, with toilets and cloakrooms, a kitchen, and a bright, light-filled space to be used for Social Hour, the Thanksgiving dinner, and other community events.

With just 40 members, the building project was a bold move. But they trusted in their future, and the power of their faith. They knew they were there to spread the good news and to provide a spiritual home for those who had been damaged by their childhood religion, for those who felt outcast by society, and for those who wanted to deepen their own lives. So they hired an architect and raised the money for the extension and debated the merits of design, and flooring, and light fixtures. They painted window frames and nailed down plywood and fed the workers. They co-ordinated with the contractor and dealt with delays and hassles and sawdust all over everything, and flooded basements. It was a miraculous time.

Now with 70 members and 40–50 in worship, a welcoming presence in the community, and a beautiful new fellowship hall, this small congregation continues to grow and be a vital place for its members and friends. This little parish church knows it is strong, and important. And it knows it will never be anything but small, and that's OK.

Prospects for further growth

What is a small congregation? Can a small congregation grow? Is being small a good thing, or a bad thing? Two-thirds of the Unitarian Universalist congregations in the United States are considered small (fewer than 150 members). These congregations are all sizes of small – from ten-member, newly emerging fellowships, to groups of fifty with 200-year-old buildings, to congregations of 125 or so, struggling with whether they are small or turning into something bigger. Some congregations have ministers in some capacity, from full time to a few hours a month; others want no clergy at all.

But, no matter their actual size, or whether they have a building or a minister, any small congregation can grow. Just how much they can grow is another question altogether. Most small congregations will always be some kind of small; maybe a quarter can become mid-size (150–500 members). So much depends on your location and demographics, as much as your welcoming energy.

In the USA we estimate that one per cent of the population within driving distance of a church are potential Unitarian Universalists. In the United Kingdom, which has a much weaker church-attending culture than the USA, the folks you can draw from will be a different proportion of the population. So look at your area with a clear eye, and make a determination:

just how many people, realistically, in your vicinity would be interested in your congregation? That's how big you can be.

Prepare for visitors

Now, it's time to plan for those visitors. First of all, all those potential UUs have to be able to find you. Do you advertise in the newspaper and the phone book? Do you have a website, an answering machine with directions, and good signage in front of your building? Is there an obvious place to park?

Then, when they find you, newcomers have to feel comfortable, welcomed, and enriched. Are your worship services spiritually growth-enhancing, or do they resemble a Sunday morning debating society? Do you have good-quality religious education for the children, child care for the little ones, and a youth group for the teenagers? Is your worship service welcoming to disabled people, young adults, elders, and bisexual, gay, lesbian, and transgender people? Is the order of service clear about when to sit and stand, what words to recite, who to talk with about certain things, and what other programmes you offer? Can people find the toilet, and is it clean? But, most of all, do the members of the congregation welcome newcomers? Are guests greeted warmly, and genuinely? Are the differences between introverts and extroverts respected? Or are people either overwhelmed or ignored before, during, and after worship? Take the time to look at your congregation with fresh eyes. Pretend you have never been there before, and ask yourself the above questions. How comfortable would you be to attend this church?

Small is still beautiful

All congregations can grow, if only to replace the members who will die or move away. By being warm, and welcoming, with a high-quality Sunday morning experience, you're on your way to healthy growth in your small congregation. And remember, *small is beautiful*. Just as with people, congregations come in all sizes and shapes. Love who you are, and what you can become, and reach out to those who are just waiting to find our message of liberal religion.

The author

Revd Jane Dwinell is the former Small Church Specialist for the Northeast District of the Unitarian Universalist Association. She is now a small-church consultant in private practice. She lives with her family in Montpelier, Vermont. She is passionate about small congregations anywhere, and helps them in any way she can. Visit http://lists.uua.org/mailman/listinfo/smalltalknewsletter to subscribe to *Small Talk,* a newsletter (published ten times a year) devoted to strengthening small Unitarian Universalist congregations through informative articles, resources, and good ideas.

Questions for reflection and discussion

1. Are there circumstances in which your congregation might benefit from hiring a part-time co-ordinator?

2. Does your Unitarian congregation deserve a greater financial commitment from members? If so, what systems or techniques might be used to achieve this?

3. What are the key elements of a 'high-quality Sunday morning experience'?

4. In what sense can small be beautiful for churches?

Appendix: The Object of the General Assembly of Unitarian and Free Christian Churches

We, the constituent congregations, affiliated societies and individual members, uniting in a spirit of mutual sympathy, co-operation, tolerance and respect; and recognising the worth and dignity of all people and their freedom to believe as their consciences dictate; and believing that truth is best served where the mind and conscience are free, acknowledge that the Object of the Assembly is:

> To promote a free and inquiring religion through the worship of God and the celebration of life; the service of humanity and respect for all creation; and the upholding of the liberal Christian tradition.

To this end, the Assembly may:

> Encourage and unite in fellowship bodies which uphold the religious liberty of their members, unconstrained by the imposition of creeds;

> Affirm the liberal religious heritage and learn from the spiritual, cultural and intellectual insights of all humanity;

> Act where necessary as the successor to the British and Foreign Unitarian Association and National Conference of Unitarian, Liberal Christian, Free Christian, Presbyterian and other Non-Subscribing or Kindred Congregations, being faithful to the spirit of their work and principles (see appendix to the constitution), providing always that this shall in no way limit the complete doctrinal freedom of the constituent churches and members of the Assembly;

> Do all other such lawful things as are incidental to the attainment of the above Object.

(Adopted at the General Assembly Annual Meetings, April 2001)

Printed in the United Kingdom
by Lightning Source UK Ltd.
112864UKS00001B/37-54